CAE
Practice Tests 2

SELF-STUD KR

Louise Hashemi

CAMBRIDGE
UNIVERSITY PRESS

Published by the Press Syndicate of the University of Cambridge
The Pitt Building, Trumpington Street, Cambridge CB2 1RP
40 West 20th Street, New York, NY 10011–4211, USA
10 Stamford Road, Oakleigh, Melbourne 3166, Australia

© Cambridge University Press 1995

First published 1995

Printed in Great Britain
at the University Press, Cambridge

ISBN 0 521 44887 5 Self-study Edition
ISBN 0 521 44886 7 Student's Book
ISBN 0 521 44888 3 Teacher's Book
ISBN 0 521 44889 1 Cassettes

19666

Contents

Thanks

I am very grateful to Paul Carne and Lynda Taylor for reading the manuscript and making many useful suggestions; to Jeanne McCarten, Geraldine Mark, Peter Ducker and especially Barbara Thomas, at Cambridge University Press, for their expert help and unflagging support; to the Subject Officers at UCLES who have so patiently answered my queries.

The author and publishers would also like to thank the teachers and students at the following institutions for piloting the material for us: The Bell School of Languages, Cambridge; The Bell College, Saffron Walden; The British Council, Athens; The British Council, Madrid; The British Institute of Florence, Italy; The British Institute, Valencia, Spain; Department of Language Studies, Christchurch College, Canterbury; Eurocentres, Cambridge; Hilderstone College, Broadstairs; International House, Hastings; International House, London; Oxford College of Further Education; St. Clare's College, Oxford; Studio School of English, Cambridge; The Swan School of English, Oxford.

To the student

This book will help you if you are preparing for the University of Cambridge Certificate in Advanced English. If you are working mostly or entirely on your own, you will find it especially helpful. It offers you practice in all five papers of the examination and gives you suggestions about how best to prepare. It also contains all the answers for the Reading, English in Use and Listening papers so that you can check your work, and some model answers for the Writing paper.

For more information about the examination and a list of centres where you can take CAE, write to: University of Cambridge Local Examinations Syndicate, 1 Hills Road, Cambridge, CB1 2EU, England.

Introduction

What is CAE?

The exam consists of five papers, each of which is worth 20% of the total marks. Here is a brief description of the five papers:

Paper 1 Reading

Time: 1 hour 15 minutes to answer the questions and transfer your answers to the answer sheet.
Structure: Four parts. Parts 1 and 4 have multiple matching questions (see p. 3). These are worth one mark each. Part 2 is multiple choice (see p. 4) and Part 3 is a gapped text (see p. 5). The questions in Parts 2 and 3 are worth two marks each. There are between 35 and 50 questions on this paper.

Paper 2 Writing

Time: 2 hours
Structure: Two parts. Section A is compulsory and you have to write everything that is asked for. You have to write one or more pieces, using some given information. You need to write about 250 words *altogether* for this part. In Section B you can choose one of four tasks. Again you'll have to write about 250 words.

Paper 3 English in Use

Time: 1 hour 30 minutes to answer the questions and transfer your answers to the answer sheet.
Structure: Six parts. Section A contains two cloze tests (see pp. 9–10), Section B has an error correction exercise and a transformation exercise (see pp. 10–11) and Section C has a multiple matching exercise (see p. 12) and a note-expansion exercise. There are about 70 questions altogether and you have to do all of them.

Paper 4 Listening

Time: About 45 minutes including the time allowed at the end to transfer your answers to the answer sheet.
Structure: Four parts. The whole paper is recorded on a cassette which plays continuously, with pauses for you to write your answers (a letter or a few words). The first, third and fourth sections are repeated, but the second is heard only once. There are about 30 – 40 questions altogether.

Paper 5 Speaking

Time: About 15 minutes
Structure: You take this with another candidate (if you don't know anyone, the exam centre will find a partner for you). There are two examiners in the

room. One tells you what to do, and the other mainly listens. You mostly talk to the other candidate although sometimes you may speak directly to the examiner. As well as talking a bit about yourself, you will be given pictures to describe and discuss.

When should I enter for CAE?

This is an **advanced** examination. If you have passed the Cambridge First Certificate in English (FCE) with a good grade, you will need *at least* six months' serious study before you have any chance of passing CAE. You don't have to take FCE of course, but you need to be sure that you aren't wasting money when you enter for CAE.

Here are a few questions you can ask yourself to see whether you have a reasonable chance of passing:

- Do you read English even when you are not studying? For example, do you ever skim through an English language newspaper or magazine, picking out articles here and there which interest you? Can you manage without a dictionary most of the time, guessing meanings as you go along?
- Do you enjoy British or American films even when they aren't dubbed or subtitled in your language?
- Can you take part in a conversation about a serious subject (such as education or the environment) and make your views clear, even though your English isn't perfect?
- Can you write 250 words of reasonably accurate English in less than an hour?

If the answer to most of these questions is 'Yes', then try Test 1 Paper 3 Section A Question 2 on p. 32. If you can fill one third of the spaces correctly, without any help, you should have a fair chance of passing CAE in a few months from now, providing you study conscientiously.
If you answered 'No' to some of the questions, then you should probably wait a little longer before entering.

Using this book

This book is divided into four parts:

- The Study Notes – these give you detailed information about all the questions and suggestions about how to tackle them as well as practical advice about the exam as a whole.
- The Practice Tests – these are the actual practice papers, which are like the ones in the real exam.
- The Key – this contains all the answers. It gives plans and model answers for Paper 2 (Writing) of Practice Test 1. You will also find the complete tapescript for each Listening paper here. (You can buy the cassette separately.)
- The Speaking Test – this consists of Study Notes which explain what will happen in the Speaking Test and the Tasks which tell you how to use the materials in the central Colour Section when you practise.

Part 1　Study Notes

PAPER 1　READING

There are always four texts on Paper 1. You may feel that there is a lot to read, but don't worry. You will find that some of the questions are actually quite easy and don't require you to think about every word of the text in detail. There are three main types of question. You can get a good idea of what you need to understand in each text by looking at the questions which go with it. It's a good idea to get into the habit of transferring your answers to the answer sheet (see p. 151) as you do each text. Don't wait until the end of the Paper, in case you run short of time. You don't want to leave any questions without an answer on the answer sheet!

Multiple matching

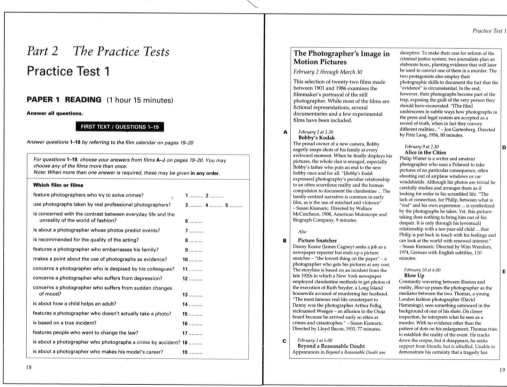

This is an example of 'multiple matching'. It is about a film guide. **You have to match the questions in the box with the films.** The questions are numbered and the films in the film guide each have a letter next to them. As there are 19 questions, but only 10 films, you will realise that you can use the same letter to answer more than one question. This isn't always the case (e.g. p. 71), so be sure to read the instructions carefully every time. **The questions come before**

the text. This is because you are supposed to read the questions first. Then you read through the text, looking out for information that gives you the answers. You can ignore quite a lot of the information. For example, you don't need to read any of the stuff about the times or dates or who directed the films because you know this is irrelevant. So save time by skipping it! **The questions are not in the same order as the information in the text** – with so many questions, that would make them too easy! So you must be prepared to jump about to find the answers.

The first and last texts on a Reading paper are always multiple matching. They often look long, but turn out to be less difficult than you expect. The best practice for these is reading for pleasure. Try to get hold of a variety of materials in English, including tourist brochures, guidebooks and magazines on subjects you're interested in. Practise reading them quickly, scanning one text and then another, in the same way as you might read in your own language.

Multiple choice

These are multiple choice questions. **You must choose the best answer for each question.** Most teachers agree that **it is better to read the text before you look at the questions.** This helps you to understand the questions better and to avoid being confused by the wrong answers. **The questions are in the same order as the information in the text,** so you can know roughly where to look for each answer. Sometimes the last question is about the text as a whole.

Gapped text

THIRD TEXT: QUESTIONS 26–31

For questions **26–31**, you must choose which of the paragraphs **A–G** match the numbered gaps in the newspaper article below. There is one extra paragraph which does not belong in any of the gaps.

BEST OF TIMES, WORST OF TIMES
RAYMOND BLANC TALKS TO DANNY DANZIGER

I thought the world was caving in, for the first time ever I lost somebody I loved; he didn't die, he just went away, but I still measure all pain by the hurt René caused me. It was a very nice childhood, an adolescence most people would wish to have, we lived in a tiny village and were a close family.

26

The adventures that children go through are the making of a friendship, building a tree house and spending a night in the forest – and losing our way back home, these things create a fantastic fabric to the friendship. There was the loving element, too, he was very caring. René was a tall bloke and very strong, and he would be my defender: if anyone ever teased me, he would be there.

27

And then at the age of 14, his family moved to the south of France, and we were in the east of France, which is 750 kilometres away ... the south of France sounded the end of the world.

28

I went quiet for the news to sink in; at first it was sheer disbelief, numbness. I couldn't sleep, and then in the night I understood the impact of the news, I understood that my life would be totally separate from his, and I had to be by myself, alone.

29

I had other friends, but never did I achieve that kind of closeness. My world completely collapsed, and nothing was the same, people, the classroom, nature, the country, butterflies.

30

He accepted that life would separate us, he didn't see it as something final, it was my dramatic side to see only the negative side, self-pity in a way. He is now living a happy life in Provence with a beautiful wife and two lovely daughters, and he is coming here next year, so it is going to be quite wonderful. It is the first time he has ever come to England, he's a good Frenchman, he does not speak a word of English.

31

It is a good, solid relationship that has been established over so many years, and has overcome all the barriers which life and time can create. I don't think it really could have lasted the way it was.

23

A   It was the finest friendship anyone could have, a brilliant pure friendship in which you would give your life for your friend. And life seemed marvellous, it seemed full of sunshine, full of incredible, beautiful things to discover, and I looked forward so much to growing up with René.

B   There is not a single bitter note, there are no power games, there is nothing secret, there is nothing which detracts from the purity of it.

Maybe because he was more mature he understood a bit better that this was part of life, that life brings people together and separates them, and distance is not necessarily the end.

D   Well our parents realised it would be very traumatic, and they did not know how to break the news, so they just announced it the day before. It was a beautiful summer's day, around five o'clock in the evening, and both parents came and said: "We are moving away, and obviously René will have to come with us."

E   Our neighbours had a son, and my wonderful childhood was shared with René; basically, we grew up together, we spent every day together, went to school together, we did all the things that children can do. It was a childhood spent in the woods, discovering the beautiful seasons, there was an abundance of produce that grew in the wild, and we went mushrooming and frog hunting, and we searched for toadstools under a full moon in winter, which we would sell because my parents didn't have much money.

F   Hopefully, we will see each other more, but it is not essential. We now have a beautifully matured, adult friendship where it is easy to talk about anything because we feel totally at ease.

G   And at that time my world stopped, it was the most incredible pain I have ever experienced, I couldn't see life without my friend, my whole system, my life, was based on René, our friendship was my life. And although he was only going away, he did not die, it was the worst loss I have ever had in my life, still, now, and 30 years later I have not received another shock of that nature.

Remember to put your answers on the separate answer sheet.

24

This is a 'gapped text'. Here the examiners want to know whether you can follow the thread of a story or explanation, using clues in the text. Some paragraphs (**A – G**) have been removed and mixed up in random order. The rest of the text is left with numbered gaps in it. **You have to fit the loose paragraphs back into the correct gaps**. There is one extra paragraph which does not belong in any of the gaps.

The best way to tackle a gapped text is to read the text, ignoring the gaps as much as possible, and **try to understand the meaning of the text as a whole**. Then go back to the beginning and consider the gaps one by one. What information is needed to bridge each gap? Look at the paragraphs **before and after** it. Then look at **A – G**. Choose one of them. Do this for each gap. Sometimes you'll feel that two of the loose paragraphs are both suitable to fill one of the gaps. If this happens, note which they are and continue. You'll probably find that one of them is needed for another gap later on, so you can eliminate it.

PAPER 2   WRITING

This paper tests your ability to write pieces such as letters, reports and short articles.

Section A

You may wonder why there is so much to read in Section A. There are two reasons. First, the examiners want to test your ability to choose important information, to ignore irrelevant information and to organise what you are writing. Second, the examiners want to give all the candidates the same opportunity to show how well they can write in English in a way that doesn't make the task easier for people who are more inventive or imaginative than others.

It's important to read the whole of Section A very carefully. It's in three parts. First there's **the background information.** This tells you about **the situation** you're in when you write. This is usually given in a few lines at the beginning. Second, there's **the text,** or more often, **texts.** These contain **the information you need to put in your answer.** Third, there is **the task,** which is **what you have to write.** This usually comes at the end, but sometimes comes between the situation and the texts. The task is often divided into more than one part. The total number of words you need to write will always be the same.

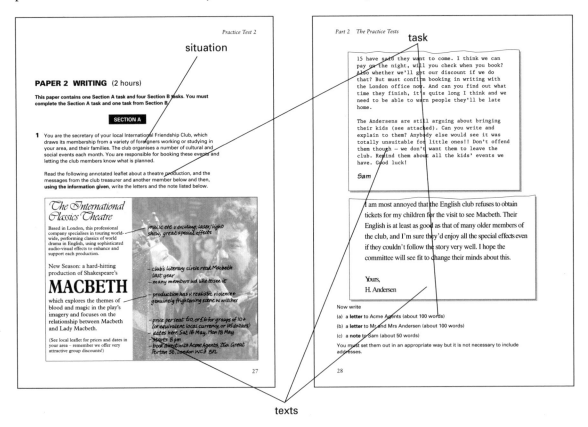

In this example, there are three texts. When you are doing Section A, it is very useful to have a highlighter pen or a pencil so that you can **mark the important points.** For each part of the task, you need to think carefully about which information is essential and which is irrelevant. Then you should **make a brief plan** (see Key p. 111).

Section B

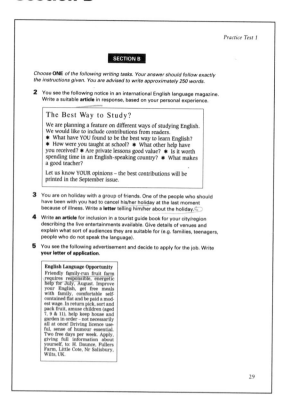

In this section, you have to **choose one of four tasks**. There is usually a good variety of things to write about and you should find something which you can tackle. Working through the tasks in this book will help you to understand the sort of **subjects** you need to be able to write about, for example:

> your home and family
> your job or school
> the area where you live
> your career plans
> how to describe yourself to a prospective
>   employer
> how to describe leisure facilities
> how to give your opinion on important
>   issues
> how to give advice
> etc.

Do try to practise *all* the different types of task, not just the ones you find easy. For example, although there is often a task which requires you to apply for a job, there isn't always, so don't count on it! Don't try to write 'perfect' answers which you hope will work however the task is worded. The examiners are very severe if they think you're 'adapting' a previously drafted answer to fit the task they've set, so you'll probably lose a lot of marks.

Planning is vital

The best way to succeed is by thorough planning, so that you know exactly what you are going to write before you start. This allows you to concentrate on producing good English while you are writing. There are sample plans in the Key (see pp. 111, 113).

How many words?

The suggested number of words means that you probably need **about 250** altogether for each section to give a good answer. If you write much more or less than this, you may lose marks because you've probably included irrelevant information or omitted something important. **Don't waste time counting words** during the exam. As part of your preparation, check what 250 words of your writing looks like. Now you have a good idea of how much you need to write and you needn't worry about it any more.

Everyone makes some mistakes

Of course, no one expects your work to be absolutely perfect. You wouldn't be taking the exam if it were, you'd be one of the examiners! However, you are expected to write good, clear, appropriate English which would have an appropriate effect on the intended reader. To help you focus your practice, it may be useful for you to know that you can lose marks for the following:

> including unnecessary details
> leaving out vital information
> poor organisation
> inappropriate register (e.g. too formal or informal)
> inaccurate grammar (especially repeated errors such as using the wrong tense)
> poor spelling
> illegible hand writing

Practice for Paper 2

In the Key (pp. 111–117), you will find plans and model answers for all the tasks on the Writing paper of Practice Test 1. These are to help you judge what is needed, especially with regard to content and organisation.

Suggestions for using this book

First stage (Practice Test 1)

- check exactly what you have to do
- note the style and tone you should use (*what* are you writing? *who* is going to read it?)
- write a plan
- compare your plan with the one in the Key
- make any changes you want to (remember, your plan may work just as well, so only make changes if there's a clear need to do so)
- write your answer (try to do this in about 40 minutes)
- read your answer through carefully to **check for mistakes**

Second stage (Practice Tests 2 – 4)

- check exactly what you have to do
- note the style and tone you should use (*what* are you writing? *who* is going to read it?)
- write a plan
- write your answer (try to do this in about 40 minutes)
- read your answer through carefully to **check for mistakes**

PAPER 3   ENGLISH IN USE

This paper tests your ability to use vocabulary and grammar accurately. There are six questions, arranged in three sections.

Section A

This section contains two cloze tests. These are texts with gaps in them. You have to put **one** word in each gap.

Question 1

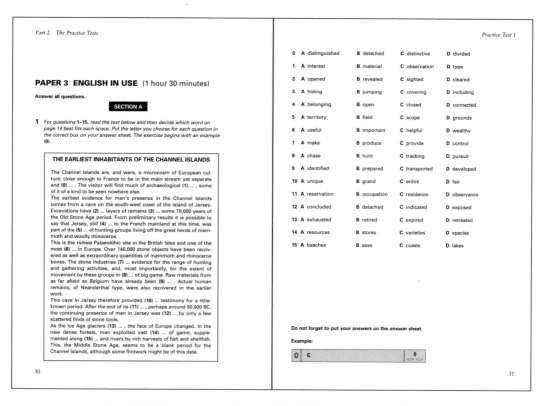

This text is mainly testing your **vocabulary**. You are given **a choice of four words** for each gap. It's a good idea to read the whole text through quickly before you start, so that you know the general subject and the style of the text, as this can help you decide which words are appropriate. Then work methodically from the beginning. Remember to **read the whole sentence** each time, not just the words in front of the gap. If you don't know, make a sensible guess, you may be right. Never leave a blank. **Blank spaces can't get marks, but guesses sometimes do!**

Question 2

This text is mainly testing your understanding of **grammar and linking words**. It looks similar to Question 1, but you are not given any words to choose from. Remember, you must use **one word only** for each gap and that word must be spelt correctly. The sort of words you need are often common words such as prepositions, adverbs or pronouns. **It is essential to read through the text before you start** and to **look at the context** of each gap when you are trying to fill it. Sometimes the clues you need are in another sentence. For example, look at gap (**19**) in *The vegetarian meal*. You can only find the right answer if you realise that the writer is **contrasting** 'to get free of stereotyped ideas' with 'falling into the trap'. If you find one gap especially difficult, it is a good idea to leave it and carry on. Sometimes when the text is almost complete you will find that the meaning becomes clearer and the missing word springs to mind almost automatically. In the end, it's always worth having a guess – you can't lose anything by doing so.

Section B

Question 3

This question is testing your ability to **spot errors**. We all make mistakes when we write and research shows that we can correct most of our own mistakes if we train ourselves to find them. So practising for this question will benefit your writing generally. The text you have to correct has **one mistake in most lines.** You are always told what sort of mistakes to look for, for example, spelling, punctuation, unnecessary words. **Read the instructions carefully and look at the example** so that you are clear what you are looking for.

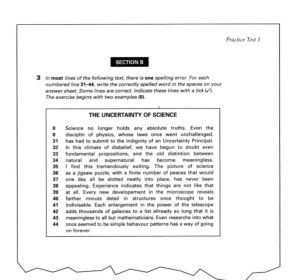

Question 4

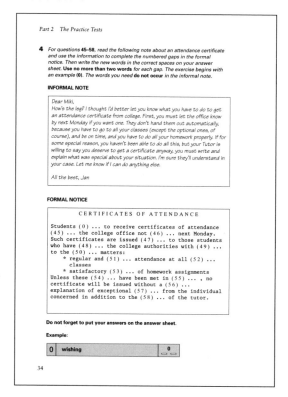

This question is testing your ability to vary **style and register**. For example, the sort of language you use when writing a note to a close friend is different from the sort you use when you are writing to someone you've never met. There are two texts. They both convey the **same information**, but they are aimed at **different readers**. You must fill the gaps in the second text so that it means the same as the first one, but using words which are appropriate to its own style and register. The first text is usually more informal, so that you have to find formal words, but sometimes they are the other way round. For this reason it is essential to **read the instructions** very carefully every time. Some gaps need **one word** and some need **two**. You have to decide about this for yourself. The words you need to use are **never in the first text,** so it's up to you to think of them. Correct spelling and accurate grammar are essential.

Do take the time to **read both texts right through before you start**. This will help you to understand the meaning and to become aware of their contrasting styles.

Section C

Question 5

This question is testing your understanding of how a text is structured. It is a bit like the gapped text on Paper 1. However, the gapped text deals with the links between parts of a text, such as paragraphs. Here, we are dealing with the way ideas are developed in sentences and carried from one sentence to another. You have to match phrases with the gaps in the text. Although this looks rather difficult, there are usually lots of clues to help you. Begin by reading the text to find out what it's about and how the ideas develop from the beginning to the end. **Notice where the gaps come**, for example, are they at the beginning of any sentences? They'll have to begin with a capital letter then, won't they? **Decide what you're looking for.** Are you looking for the subject of a sentence? An expression of time? A verb? The answers to these questions will help you to narrow the number of possibilities.

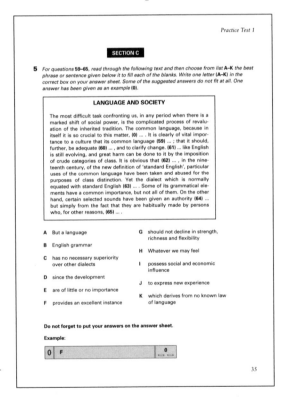

In the example (0) given in *Language and Society*, we are clearly looking for a verb to go with the words 'The common language' and we need a phrase which will complete the sentence. So we know immediately that **A, B, D, H, J** and **K** cannot be the answer, as they are the wrong sort of phrase. **E** and **I** are plural, so they won't fit. So we must choose the best meaning from **C** or **F**. **C** makes no sense here (what 'other dialects'?), but **F** does, especially if we remember to look at the following sentence.

Question 6

Part 2   The Practice Tests

6 Use the following notes to write instructions for visitors to a holiday cottage. Write **one complete sentence** on the answer sheet for each numbered set of notes, using connecting words and phrases as appropriate. You may add words and change the form of the words given in the notes but do not add any extra information. The first point has been expanded for you as an example **(0)**.

Ocean Ridge Cottage

0   Keys available from Mr Boyce, contact at Lazy Cat Cafe
81 Hire car booked (Bristows, garage opposite station) deposit (£25) payable on collection
82 From Bristows: left (Station Rd), follow Coast Road (clearly signed) 3 km, Ocean Ridge cottage top of hill
83 Water already connected, electricity meter behind door (£1 coins)
84 Phone – incoming calls only – in hall
85 NB path from back door to beach very steep, supervise children, cottage owner not responsible accidents
86 Lock cottage when out, unfortunately frequent theft from holiday homes recently – cash, credit cards, cameras etc.

The space below can be used for your rough answers.
Do not forget to put your answers on the answer sheet.

0	The keys are available from Mr Boyce, who can be contacted at the Lazy Cat Cafe.
81	
82	
83	
84	
85	
86	

36

This question is testing your ability to produce very clear, **accurate** English. Notes have many words missing which we would expect to find in normal spoken or written language and they may include abbreviations. You have to **expand each numbered note into one full sentence.** The sort of words you have to add will be *a, the, some, which, who, that, is, are, should, has, have, in, on, by* etc. You **mustn't add new information.** Sometimes you need to **change the form of words** given in the notes, for example, in *Ocean Ridge Cottage*, 'contact' becomes 'can be contacted'. Make sure you **don't change the meaning** of the notes. Concentrate on writing grammatically accurate English.

PAPER 4   LISTENING

This paper tests your ability to understand spoken English. You will listen to a cassette tape and you have to write your answers. The tapescripts are printed in full in the Key (e.g. see pp. 119, 125, 131, 138), to help you to understand the answers when you are checking your work. For practice you really need to hear the recording. You can buy the tape to go with this book if you do not have access to one in a school or library. Try to listen to as much spoken English as you can. One way to do this is to tune in to English language radio broadcasts in your country. For details of British overseas broadcasts, write to BBC, Bush House, PO Box 76, The Strand London WC2 4PH. Ask about programmes aimed at people studying English, as well as the usual programmes. There may also be USA or Australian stations in some areas.

Section A

In this section you will hear mainly factual information. There is usually one main speaker. Sometimes the speaker is giving a talk to an audience. You have to fill spaces in notes. You can get clues from the notes which will help you predict what sort of information you need to fill the spaces. For example, if you look at *Lampley and District Museum*, you can see that gaps **1** and **2** probably need a descriptive word (important? many? strange?), whereas gap **3** needs the name of something or somebody and gap **4** needs a period of time. Practise finding clues like these in the pause before the speaker begins. You hear this section twice, which gives you a chance to catch anything you missed the first time around.

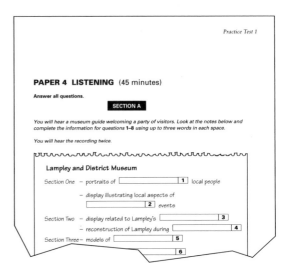

Section B

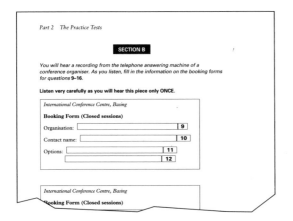

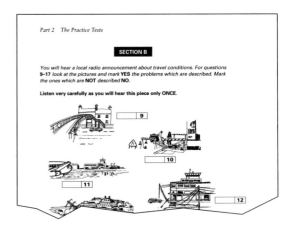

This section is a bit like Section A, but the language tends to be a little simpler, because you only hear it once. There is no repeat. You must complete your answers with one hearing. Sometimes you have to complete notes, sometimes you have to mark answers 'Yes' or 'No'. Again, as with Section A, you can find a lot of useful clues in the questions, and you should use the pause to prepare yourself as thoroughly as you can.

Section C

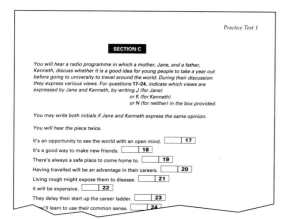

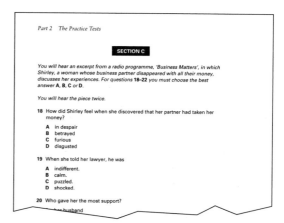

In this section you are being tested mainly on people's opinions and attitudes. There are usually two or three speakers. Sometimes you have to show that you understand which speaker expressed a particular opinion. See the example above. Sometimes there are multiple choice questions. Sometimes you have to complete sentences or notes. Again, use the questions to help you understand what you hear. You always hear this section twice.

Section D

In this section, you will hear five different speakers. There are two tasks. Both of them are matching tasks. For example, you may have to match each speaker with a job and then listen again to match each speaker with an opinion. There is a link between what the different speakers are saying. For example, they may be talking about a similar topic, or they may be talking about the same event. This section may look confusing until you have tried it, but once you've had some practice, it's not so difficult. Don't forget to use the questions as clues to help you listen for the right information.

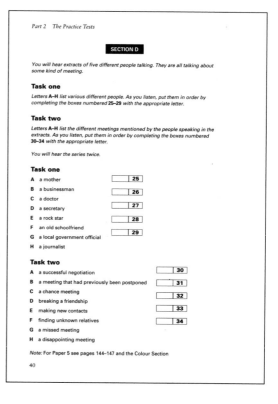

TAKING THE EXAM

Some time before the exam takes place, you will be told the dates of your exam, and where you have to be at what time. Papers 1, 2 and 3 take place on one day. Papers 4 and 5 will probably take place on one or two different days. Make sure you follow the instructions carefully and arrive in good time.

WRITING YOUR ANSWERS

For Papers 1, 3 and 4 you will be provided with special answer sheets. You should study the samples at the back of this book carefully and make sure that you understand how to use them. Many people prefer to mark their answers on the question papers and then copy them onto the answer sheet later. This works well for Papers 3 and 4, but it is not such a good idea for Paper 1 (see below).

Paper 1

	A B C D E F G H I J		A B C D E F G H I J		A B C D E F G H I J
1		21		41	
2	A B C D E F G H I J	22	A B C D E F G H I J	42	A B C D E F G H I J
3	A B C D E F G H I J	23	A B C D E F G H I J	43	A B C D E F G H I J

For paper 1 you need a soft pencil and a good quality eraser. This shows the answers marked in for Questions 1 and 2 of Practice Test 1 Paper 1 (see p. 18). The answer for Question 1 is E and the answer for Question 2 is J. These marks **must** be made in **pencil**. If you change your mind, **you can rub out your answer.** Be sure to do this **cleanly.** This answer sheet will be 'read' by an electronic eye and any dirty marks may be misinterpreted by it.

You may notice that **1** and **2** are both answers to the same question. Because of this, it doesn't matter which answer you give first. This is quite often the case with multiple matching questions and you will find that in the Key such answers are marked 'interchangeable'.

When you do a multiple choice text, you will realise that you are only choosing **A, B, C** or **D**, but the answer sheet offers you **E – J** as well. Don't worry about this, just ignore the unnecessary letters.

If possible, practise filling the answer sheet while you are answering the questions on Paper 1, don't wait to copy your answers at the end. (Remember, you are allowed to photocopy the answer sheets at the end of this book, so you can have plenty of practice with them.) There are two reasons why it's better to write straight onto the answer sheet. First, you **save time**, which is usually important on Paper 1. Second, you **avoid errors** in copying.

Paper 2

You must write your answers for Paper 2 on the paper provided for you. You **must** write in **pen** and you must hand in all your rough notes and plans at the end of the test. If you want to change something, cross it out neatly. Don't use brackets ( ) for this. Write as clearly as possible. This paper is marked by human beings and tidy, legible work is much appreciated! Really bad handwriting can actually lose marks, if the examiner has to struggle to read it.

Paper 3 and Paper 4

57	circumstances	57	59	G	59
58	recommendation	58	60	J	60

For these papers, it is quite a good idea to **write your answers on the question paper** and then **transfer** them to the special answer sheet. There is usually plenty of time during Paper 3 to do this and for Paper 4 you are given ten minutes at the end of the test. It's best to write in **pen** although you can use pencil. Be careful not to make spelling mistakes when you are copying. Be careful not to make any other marks on the answer sheet. Your answers will be marked correct or incorrect on this sheet, and then the electronic eye will count your marks.

Note: The answers for Paper 3 Question 6 (**81** etc.) go on the **back** of the answer sheet in the special long spaces.

RESULTS

When you receive your result, you will be given a grade for the whole exam. The highest grade is A, the lowest is E. If you get A, B or C, you have passed. If you get D or E, you have failed. If you pass the exam, your results slip will show if you did particularly well in some papers. For example it might show that your exam grade is B (well done!), but you actually scored A on Papers 1 and 3 (very well done indeed!). If you fail the exam, your results slip will show you in which papers you did badly. This will help you if you decide to try again, because you will know where you need the most practice.

Part 2   The Practice Tests

Practice Test 1

PAPER 1 READING (1 hour 15 minutes)

Answer all questions.

FIRST TEXT / QUESTIONS 1–19

*Answer questions **1–19** by referring to the film calendar on pages 19–20*

> For questions **1–19**, choose your answers from films **A–J** on pages 19–20. You may choose any of the films more than once.
> Note: When more than one answer is required, these may be given **in any order**.

Which film or films

feature photographers who try to solve crimes?	**1** .... **2** ....
use photographs taken by real professional photographers?	**3** .... **4** .... **5** ....
is concerned with the contrast between everyday life and the unreality of the world of fashion?	**6** ....
is about a photographer whose photos predict events?	**7** ....
is recommended for the quality of the acting?	**8** ....
features a photographer who embarrasses his family?	**9** ....
makes a point about the use of photographs as evidence?	**10** ....
concerns a photographer who is despised by his colleagues?	**11** ....
concerns a photographer who suffers from depression?	**12** ....
concerns a photographer who suffers from sudden changes of mood?	**13** ....
is about how a child helps an adult?	**14** ....
features a photographer who doesn't actually take a photo?	**15** ....
is based on a true incident?	**16** ....
features people who want to change the law?	**17** ....
is about a photographer who photographs a crime by accident?	**18** ....
is about a photographer who makes his model's career?	**19** ....

The Photographer's Image in Motion Pictures

February 2 through March 30

This selection of twenty-two films made between 1901 and 1986 examines the filmmaker's portrayal of the still photographer. While most of the films are fictional representations, several documentaries and a few experimental films have been included.

A

February 2 at 2.30
Bobby's Kodak
The proud owner of a new camera, Bobby eagerly snaps shots of his family at every awkward moment. When he finally displays his pictures, the whole clan is enraged, especially Bobby's father who puts an end to the new hobby once and for all. "[*Bobby's Kodak* expresses] photography's peculiar relationship to an often scurrilous reality and the human compulsion to document the clandestine ... The family-centred narrative is common in early film, as is the use of mischief and violence" – Susan Kismaric. Directed by Wallace McCutcheon, 1908, American Mutoscope and Biograph Company, 9 minutes.

Also

B

Picture Snatcher
Danny Keane (James Cagney) seeks a job as a newspaper reporter but ends up a picture snatcher – "the lowest thing on the paper" – a photographer who gets his pictures at any cost. The storyline is based on an incident from the late 1920s in which a New York newspaper employed clandestine methods to get photos of the execution of Ruth Snyder, a Long Island housewife accused of murdering her husband. "The most famous real-life counterpart to Danny was the photographer Arthur Fellig, nicknamed Weegee – an allusion to the Ouija board because he arrived early so often at crimes and catastrophes." – Susan Kismaric. Directed by Lloyd Bacon, 1933, 77 minutes.

C

February 3 at 6.00
Beyond a Reasonable Doubt
Appearances in *Beyond a Reasonable Doubt* are deceptive. To make their case for reform of the criminal justice system, two journalists plan an elaborate hoax, planting evidence that will later be used to convict one of them in a murder. The two protagonists also employ their photographic skills to document the fact that the "evidence" is circumstantial. In the end, however, their photographs become part of the trap, exposing the guilt of the very person they should have exonerated. "[The film] underscores in subtle ways how photographs in the press and legal system are accepted as a record of truth, when in fact they convey different realities..." – Jon Gartenberg. Directed by Fritz Lang, 1956, 80 minutes.

D

February 9 at 2.30
Alice in the Cities
Philip Winter is a writer and amateur photographer who uses a Polaroid to take pictures of no particular consequence, often shooting out of airplane windows or car windshields. Although his photos are trivial he carefully studies and arranges them as if looking for order in his scrambled life. "The lack of connection, for Philip, between what is "real" and his own experience ... is symbolized by the photographs he takes. Yet, this picture-taking does nothing to bring him out of his despair. It is only through his [eventual] relationship with a ten-year-old child ... that Philip is put back in touch with his feelings and can look at the world with renewed interest." – Susan Kismaric. Directed by Wim Wenders, 1974, German with English subtitles, 110 minutes.

E

February 10 at 6.00
Blow Up
Constantly wavering between illusion and reality, *Blow-up* poses the photographer as the mediator between the two. Thomas, a young London fashion photographer (David Hemmings), sees something untoward in the background of one of his shots. On closer inspection, he interprets what he sees as a murder. With no evidence other than the pattern of dots on his enlargement, Thomas tries to establish the reality of the event. He tracks down the corpse, but it disappears; he seeks support from friends, but is rebuffed. Unable to demonstrate his certainty that a tragedy has

occurred, Thomas's sense of reality is undermined, and he concedes, finally, to illusion. Directed by Michelangelo Antonioni, 1966, 110 minutes.

F   *February 24 at 6.00*
Funny Face
The musical *Funny Face* was inspired by the career of photographer Richard Avedon who, in fact, served as a consultant, and whose photographs are used in the film. The Avedon character is Dick Avery (played by Fred Astaire). One day Avery discovers the winsome, introspective Jo (Audrey Hepburn) in a Greenwich Village bookshop and in spite of her initial reluctance, transforms her through his professional artistry into a glamorous fashion model. Directed by Stanley Donen, 1957, 103 minutes.

Also

G   **Love as Disorder (An Affair of the Skin)**
Photographer Helen Levitt was the producer of this little-known work by Ben Maddow. (Levitt's photographs are also incorporated into the film.) The story revolves around five New Yorkers immersed in interlocking relationships. Viveca Lindfors, as the leading character Victoria, delivers a delicate and perceptive performance as an ageing fashion model caught against her will in a fruitless love affair. Janice (Diana Sands), temperamental photographer, is her friend and confidante. Eugene Archer, reviewing the film for the *New York Times*, noted: "The New York photography of this moderately budgeted film is outstanding, and the remaining technical credits are thoroughly expert. The acting, too, is uniformly skilled by an eminently professional cast." Directed by Ben Maddow, 1963, 102 minutes.

H   *March 3 at 6.00*
Model
In contrast to *Funny Face*, *Model* presents some of the more hard-boiled, less glamorous aspects of fashion photography. Photographers, models, and agents engage in their routine daily work – interviews, fittings, rehearsals, shows, commercials. "Wiseman's clear eye perceives wider significance ... in this apparently hermetic and self-absorbed little world: reflections on the moralities of the business ... on the dedication to create a world of beautiful fantasy which, from time to time and without commentary, he compares to the real world outside the studios and offices and salons." – David Robinson. Directed by Frederick Wiseman, 1980, 129 minutes.

I   *March 9 at 2.00*
The Eyes of Laura Mars
Laura Mars (Faye Dunaway) is a successful New York fashion photographer who specializes in modish compositions in the style of Helmut Newton (whose photographs, in fact, are used). As the film unfolds, a curious phenomenon begins to emerge: tragic events are foreshadowed in Laura's photographs, suggesting that she, the artist, has the psychic ability to "see" things before they happen. "Laura personifies a fantasy image of the photographer as an omnipotent and omnipresent force in the real world ... the eye of Laura's mind is more omniscient than the eye of the camera ..." – Jon Gartenberg. Directed by Irvin Kershner, 1978, 103 minutes.

J   *March 10 at 6.00*
Rear Window
L.B. Jefferies (Jimmy Stewart) is a news photographer confined to his Greenwich Village apartment with a broken leg. He spends his days and nights peering at his neighbours through his back window which functions for him like a camera's field of vision. With help from one of the tools of his trade – a huge telephoto lens which, ironically, he never uses to take a picture – Jefferies gradually focuses in on what appears to be a murder, and attempts to gather evidence to solve the crime. As if expressing empathy for his protagonist's immobile state, Hitchcock's own lens observes all the action of the film from the single vantage point of Jefferies' apartment. Directed by Alfred Hitchcock, 1954, 112 minutes.

Remember to put your answers on the separate answer sheet.

*Read the following newspaper article and answer questions **20–25** which follow.*

How trees are killing our rivers

In the past decade, acid rain has caused a drop in water quality in almost 60 miles of Welsh rivers. A much greater length of small tributary streams has been equally degraded. Most of the streams flow through plantations of conifer trees.

Now, it seems many of the same streams are facing another problem. The shading effect of the dark, densely planted conifer crops is altering water temperatures, causing a considerable decline in the development of many aquatic invertebrates and fish.

Anything that affects stream invertebrates and fish has a knock-on effect for other groups of animals such as otters and the characteristic birds of upland waters – dippers, grey wagtails and common sandpipers, in particular.

An assessment of the impact of conifer plantations, which now cover a quarter of the hills and uplands of Wales, on stream water temperatures has been made by Neil Weatherley and Stephen Ormerod, of the University of Wales College, Cardiff.

They studied year-round temperature variations in six streams, all of which run into the River Tywi in central Wales. Three of the rivers drained open moorland; the other three drained large plantations of 30-year-old sitka spruce, the most commonly planted conifer in these hills. Two of the spruce plantations had their trees cut down in a band 45 feet wide either side of the stream so that their shading effect on the water was at least slightly reduced. In the other plantation-draining streams, the conifers grew right to its banks. All three conifer-forested streams, like many of their counterparts in the Welsh hills, were without fish and supported

only a few varieties of aquatic invertebrates. Acidification – made worse by conifer plantations whose needle-shaped leaves effectively filter pollutants out of the air – is the likely cause. Most of the streams formerly supported good populations of brown trout and Atlantic salmon.

Doctors Weatherley and Ormerod found that average daily water temperatures between April and August were between 0.6°C and 2.8°C higher in moorland streams compared with the totally forested stream. In the winter, the pattern was reversed. Then the forested stream water was up to 0.9°C warmer. Water temperatures in the streams in the conifer plantations with trees growing well back from the banks were between those of the open moorland streams and the stream which was completely forested. Their water became up to 1°C warmer between May and June compared with the forested stream.

Temperature differences were

mainly the result of trees shading out both direct and indirect sunlight. Because their trees are so closely spaced, conifer plantations are highly effective at blocking sunlight while small streams are much more susceptible to shading effects than larger rivers.

Based on the substantial changes in water temperature caused by the planting of conifers, Doctors Weatherley and Ormerod then used published biological models – developed from laboratory studies – to simulate the impact on invertebrate and fish development.

According to these simulations, the eggs of mayfly species developed faster in a moorland stream than in a forested stream. Eggs of the common mayfly, for instance, hatched about 19 days earlier in a moorland stream after having been fertilised in the spring. This, combined with predicted faster growth of the hatched nymphs, means adults would emerge during November in a forested stream but before the end of October in a moorland stream.

Similar effects to those forecast for mayflies were predicted for brown trout by the models. Trout eggs took up to nine days longer to hatch in forested streams. Subsequent fish growth was faster in the moorland stream; a little under a year from egg fertilisation the previous November, moorland stream trout were predicted to be between 22 per cent and 39 per cent heavier than fish in forest streams.

By the end of the second growing season the effect still held, even though weight loss over winter was less in the forested stream (because its winter water temperature was slightly higher). Smaller fish are unlikely to be as fertile. Trout in streams where the conifers had been felled from the banks did virtually as well as those in moorland streams.

Doctors Weatherley and Ormerod are quick to point out the possible pitfalls of this sort of biological modelling. Numerous assumptions had to be made along the way. For instance, water temperature was measured using thermistor probes in the water flow. This works well for organisms with life stages in the surface water. On the stream bed and among the bed gravels, however, temperatures vary less than at the stream surface. Deeper down in the gravels and mud, temperatures can be more stable still – and even more different from those near the surface.

It was also assumed that no other environmental variable apart from temperature was limiting organism development.

The modelling suggests that temperature changes brought about by putting dense conifer plantations close to streams may have important consequences for stream life, similar to "moving" the stream to a colder climate, either by shifting it north or its altitude upwards.

20 How have Welsh streams been affected by flowing through conifer plantations?

  A   They carry a smaller volume of water than formerly.
  B   The water temperature is different.
  C   The fish are smaller.
  D   There are no birds living around them.

21 How many densely-shaded streams did Weatherley and Ormerod study?

  A six   **B** three   **C** two   **D** one

22 What did they discover about temperature variation in streams?

  A   There is less variation in the most densely-shaded streams.
  B   The amount of shade has little impact.
  C   Shade only affects streams in summer.
  D   Streams in open land are cooler in summer.

23 How did Weatherley and Ormerod predict the effect of conifer plantations on animal life in streams?

  A   They combined published information and their own results.
  B   They observed a variety of living creatures in streams.
  C   They made mathematical calculations based on laboratory observations.
  D   They carried out a new type of laboratory experiment.

24 What did they discover about fish in densely-shaded streams?

  A   They were infertile.
  B   They differed little from those in moorland streams.
  C   They maintained their weight better in winter.
  D   They grew faster.

25 What did Weatherley and Ormerod conclude about streams from their study?

  A   Temperature alone affects the development of living creatures.
  B   Deep streams have more variety of living creatures.
  C   Dense shading has a similar effect to climatic changes.
  D   Altitude has less effect than vegetation.

Remember to put your answers on the separate answer sheet.

THIRD TEXT: QUESTIONS 26–31

For questions 26–31, you must choose which of the paragraphs A–G match the numbered gaps in the newspaper article below. There is one extra paragraph which does not belong in any of the gaps.

BEST OF TIMES, WORST OF TIMES

RAYMOND BLANC TALKS TO DANNY DANZIGER

I thought the world was caving in, for the first time ever I lost somebody I loved; he didn't die, he just went away, but I still measure all pain by the hurt René caused me. It was a very nice childhood, an adolescence most people would wish to have, we lived in a tiny village and were a close family.

26

The adventures that children go through are the making of a friendship, building a tree house and spending a night in the forest – and losing our way back home, these things create a fantastic fabric to the friendship. There was the loving element, too, he was very caring. René was a tall bloke and very strong, and he would be my defender: if anyone ever teased me, he would be there.

27

And then at the age of 14, his family moved to the south of France, and we were in the east of France, which is 750 kilometres away ... the south of France sounded the end of the world.

28

I went quiet for the news to sink in; at first it was sheer disbelief, numbness. I couldn't sleep, and then in the night I understood the impact of the news, I understood that my life would be totally separate from his, and I had to be by myself, alone.

29

I had other friends, but never did I achieve that kind of closeness. My world completely collapsed, and nothing was the same, people, the classroom, nature, the country, butterflies.

30

He accepted that life would separate us, he didn't see it as something final, it was my dramatic side to see only the negative side, self-pity in a way. He is now living a happy life in Provence with a beautiful wife and two lovely daughters, and he is coming here next year, so it is going to be quite wonderful. It is the first time he has ever come to England, he's a good Frenchman, he does not speak a word of English.

31

It is a good, solid relationship that has been established over so many years, and has overcome all the barriers which life and time can create. I don't think it really could have lasted the way it was.

A   It was the finest friendship anyone could have, a brilliant pure friendship in which you would give your life for your friend. And life seemed marvellous, it seemed full of sunshine, full of incredible, beautiful things to discover, and I looked forward so much to growing up with René.

B   There is not a single bitter note, there are no power games, there is nothing secret, there is nothing which detracts from the purity of it.

C   Maybe because he was more mature he understood a bit better that this was part of life, that life brings people together and separates them, and distance is not necessarily the end.

D   Well our parents realised it would be very traumatic, and they did not know how to break the news, so they just announced it the day before. It was a beautiful summer's day, around five o'clock in the evening, and both parents came and said: "We are moving away, and obviously René will have to come with us."

E   Our neighbours had a son, and my wonderful childhood was shared with René; basically, we grew up together, we spent every day together, went to school together, we did all the things that children can do. It was a childhood spent in the woods, discovering the beautiful seasons, there was an abundance of produce that grew in the wild, and we went mushrooming and frog hunting, and we searched for toadstools under a full moon in winter, which we would sell because my parents didn't have much money.

F   Hopefully, we will see each other more, but it is not essential. We now have a beautifully matured, adult friendship where it is easy to talk about anything because we feel totally at ease.

G   And at that time my world stopped, it was the most incredible pain I have ever experienced, I couldn't see life without my friend, my whole system, my life, was based on René, our friendship *was* my life. And although he was only going away, he did not die, it was the worst loss I have ever had in my life, still, now, and 30 years later I have not received another shock of that nature.

Remember to put your answers on the separate answer sheet.

FOURTH TEXT / QUESTIONS 32–45

Answer questions **32–45** by referring to the entries from a guide to Italian hotels on pages 25–26.

For questions **32–45** match the statements below to the guide book entries **A–H**. Some of the statements apply to more than one entry.

Note: When more than one answer is required, these may be given **in any order**.

Although the hotel looks rather grand the atmosphere is relaxed.	32 ....
Some of the bedrooms are not very comfortable.	33 .... 34 ....
	35 ....
You don't pay a lot extra for a room with a good view.	36 ....
The dining-room is quite ordinary.	37 ....
This hotel sounds comfortable rather than smart.	38 ....
It doesn't sound as if the staff are very helpful.	39 ....
This hotel is in fact a group of buildings.	40 ....
This hotel is not very cheap but it represents good value for money.	41 .... 42 ....
You can enjoy sitting outdoors right by the water.	43 .... 44 ....
The remains of medieval decorations are still visible here.	45 ....

Italian Hotels

A   The original building of this hotel, which now houses reception, breakfast rooms and a few bedrooms, dates back to the Middle Ages, when it was a farmhouse. To this have been added little detached chalets with kitchen facilities, and a separate restaurant. Despite these alterations, however, much of the charm of the old building has been retained. The breakfast rooms have simple, rustic furniture and traces of the original decorative paintings on the panelled walls. Antiques are dotted around, with plenty of fresh flowers.

B   It is odd to walk into this small old villa on the shore of Lake Como and find an English-style bar upholstered in tartan. But when you meet the jolly owner and discover that his wife is a Scot, the friendly British guest-house atmosphere is explained. In the sitting-room (with views out over the lake), the old painted ceiling remains, and antiques are scattered around. The bedrooms are simply, even basically, furnished and some are a little cramped; those at the back are possibly rather noisy, but those at the front have splendid views of the lake.

   There is little point in staying in Arona without views of Lake Maggiore, and this hotel's great attraction is a large terrace shaded by a magnificent awning of well-trained wisteria, looking across the road to the waterfront. Rooms (with lake views for a modest premium) have been decorated with a modest attempt at individuality – for example tartan carpets, marble tops, brass and china lamp fittings. The dining-room is strictly average in ambience and decoration, but in season there will be the Piedmontese speciality of local mushrooms in several guises. It is a family business with friendly, willing staff. **C**

   Mario Ortelli represents the third generation of his family to run this popular little hotel on the shores of Lake Lugano. Bedrooms are large, and have appar- **D** ently been prettily refurbished; the little sitting-room has a pleasantly lived-in atmosphere, with pictures, comfy furniture and books – many in English. But the most appealing feature is the slightly unkempt garden and gravelled terrace, shaded by pergolas, which juts right into the lake.

E

Driving along the N11 highway from Padua to Venice, you follow an old canal whose banks are scattered with beautiful 18thC villas, where wealthy Venetians used to escape the heat and stench of the city in the summer months. This hotel is one of them – surrounded by calm formal gardens, with statues, a fountain, ancient trees and arbours.

The entrance to the hotel is rather grand. The marble-floored reception area leads into a vast chandeliered dining-hall, with a more modest breakfast room to one side. In the bedrooms, much of the furniture is antique and in some the original softly painted walls and ceilings remain. The larger rooms have balconies and all are of a generous size. The smaller rooms at the rear overlook horse chestnut trees.

The welcome and service are not a strong point. When we last visited, no dinner was available because the chef had driven off the road. We had no complaint about that, but no attempt was made to make alternative dinner arrangements.

F

Book weeks in advance and you might just be lucky enough to get a room at this hotel. Though it is not quite the bargain it used to be, it is still a place of immense charm and character with prices that most people can afford and a very convenient but tranquil location. But what really distinguishes the hotel is its garden – the spacious patio beside the canal, where tables are scattered among potted plants and classical urns, and the grassy garden at the back where wisteria, roses and fruit trees flourish.

It is thanks to the Marzollo family, who have been here since 1955, that the aristocratic charm of the villa has been preserved. There are still touches of grandeur, and the furnishings for the most part are classically Venetian. But there is no trace whatever of formality.

Reception is a spacious hallway-cum-salon, with ample seating, stretching between two gardens. Most of the bedrooms are rather old-fashioned, with a haphazard collection of antiques. Some are surprisingly spartan, and those on the upper floor are quite modern in style.

G

A sweeping, tree-lined drive leading through lawns with lofty palms to a fine late Renaissance mansion set against thickly wooded hills; then, an interior no less splendid – frescoes embellishing every inch of wall and ceiling, handsome classical busts on ornate stands, antiques, chandeliers and, from the 16thC salon and its balcony, a beautiful view of the sloping lawns below. Ruinously expensive? For once, no: all of this comes for less than you pay for a room in some seedy station hotel.

The bedrooms are not quite so grand, which accounts for the strikingly low prices. In fact the cheapest are bordering on the basic. The best doubles have touches of grandeur, however.

The old cellars serve as the breakfast room, where framed awards and the colossal terracotta urn are clues to the basis of the 19thC success of the estate: top-quality olive oil.

H

This hotel is unrivalled in Turin: a noble villa, dating from the early 17th century and retaining many of the original features – marble floors, ornately carved doors, old fireplaces, 17thC candelabra and Old Master paintings on the walls – set in glorious wooded grounds. The bedrooms are furnished with antiques and look out over the park.

There is also an impressive restaurant, now part of a chain, with the option of eating on the lawns under grand parasols. Staying here, if you can afford it, is very much part of the experience of visiting Turin.

PAPER 2 WRITING (2 hours)

This paper contains one Section A task and four Section B tasks. You must
complete the Section A task and one task from Section B.

1 You are the secretary of your local International Friendship Club, which
draws its membership from a variety of foreigners working or studying in
your area, and their families. The club organises a number of cultural and
social events each month. You are responsible for booking these events and
letting the club members know what is planned.

Read the following annotated leaflet about a theatre production, and the
messages from the club treasurer and another member below and then,
using the information given, write the letters and the note listed below.

The International Classics Theatre

Based in London, this professional
company specialises in touring world-
wide, performing classics of world
drama in English, using sophisticated
audio-visual effects to enhance and
support each production.

New Season: a hard-hitting
production of Shakespeare's

MACBETH

which explores the themes of
blood and magic in the play's
imagery and focuses on the
relationship between Macbeth
and Lady Macbeth.

(See local leaflet for prices and dates in
your area – remember we offer very
attractive group discounts!)

Annotations:

- music etc v. exciting; laser/light show; great special effects

- club's literary circle read Macbeth last year
- many members wd like to see it

- production has v. realistic violence + genuinely frightening scene w. witches

- price per seat £10, or £6 for groups of 10+ (or equivalent local currency, or US dollars)
- dates here Sat 16 May, Mon 18 May
- starts 8 pm
- book direct with Acme Agents, 25a Great Porton St, London WC3 8FL

15 have said they want to come. I think we can pay on the night, will you check when you book? Also whether we'll get our discount if we do that? But must confirm booking in writing with the London office now. And can you find out what time they finish, it's quite long I think and we need to be able to warn people they'll be late home.

The Andersens are still arguing about bringing their kids (see attached). Can you write and explain to them? Anybody else would see it was totally unsuitable for little ones!! Don't offend them though — we don't want them to leave the club. Remind them about all the kids' events we have. Good luck!

Sam

I am most annoyed that the English club refuses to obtain tickets for my children for the visit to see Macbeth. Their English is at least as good as that of many older members of the club, and I'm sure they'd enjoy all the special effects even if they couldn't follow the story very well. I hope the committee will see fit to change their minds about this.

Yours,
H. Andersen

Now write

(a) a **letter** to Acme Agents (about 100 words)

(b) a **letter** to Mr and Mrs Andersen (about 100 words)

(c) a **note** to Sam (about 50 words)

You must set them out in an appropriate way but it is not necessary to include addresses.

SECTION B

*Choose **ONE** of the following writing tasks. Your answer should follow exactly the instructions given. You are advised to write approximately 250 words.*

2 You see the following notice in an international English language magazine. Write a suitable **article** in response, based on your personal experience.

The Best Way to Study?

We are planning a feature on different ways of studying English. We would like to include contributions from readers.
* What have YOU found to be the best way to learn English?
* How were you taught at school? * What other help have you received? * Are private lessons good value? * Is it worth spending time in an English-speaking country? * What makes a good teacher?

Let us know YOUR opinions – the best contributions will be printed in the September issue.

---

3 You are on holiday with a group of friends. One of the people who should have been with you had to cancel his/her holiday at the last moment because of illness. Write a **letter** telling him/her about the holiday.

4 Write **an article** for inclusion in a tourist guide book for your city/region describing the live entertainments available. Give details of venues and explain what sort of audiences they are suitable for (e.g. families, teenagers, people who do not speak the language).

5 You see the following advertisement and decide to apply for the job. Write **your letter of application**.

English Language Opportunity

Friendly family-run fruit farm requires responsible, energetic help for July, August. Improve your English, get free meals with family, comfortable self-contained flat and be paid a modest wage. In return pick, sort and pack fruit, amuse children (aged 7, 9 & 11), help keep house and garden in order – not necessarily all at once! Driving licence useful, sense of humour essential. Two free days per week. Apply, giving full information about yourself, to: H. Daunce, Fullers Farm, Little Cote, Nr Salisbury, Wilts, UK.

PAPER 3 ENGLISH IN USE (1 hour 30 minutes)

Answer all questions.

SECTION A

1 *For questions* **1–15**, *read the text below and then decide which word on page 14 best fits each space. Put the letter you choose for each question in the correct box on your answer sheet. The exercise begins with an example* **(0)**.

THE EARLIEST INHABITANTS OF THE CHANNEL ISLANDS

The Channel Islands are, and were, a microcosm of European culture; close enough to France to be in the main stream yet separate and **(0)** ... . The visitor will find much of archaeological **(1)** ... , some of it of a kind to be seen nowhere else.

The earliest evidence for man's presence in the Channel Islands comes from a cave on the south-west coast of the island of Jersey. Excavations have **(2)** ... layers of remains **(3)** ... some 70,000 years of the Old Stone Age period. From preliminary results it is possible to say that Jersey, still **(4)** ... to the French mainland at this time, was part of the **(5)** ... of hunting-groups living off the great herds of mammoth and woolly rhinoceros.

This is the richest Palaeolithic site in the British Isles and one of the most **(6)** ... in Europe. Over 140,000 stone objects have been recovered as well as extraordinary quantities of mammoth and rhinoceros bones. The stone industries **(7)** ... evidence for the range of hunting and gathering activities, and, most importantly, for the extent of movement by these groups in **(8)** ... of big game. Raw materials from as far afield as Belgium have already been **(9)** ... . Actual human remains, of Neanderthal type, were also recovered in the earlier work.

This cave in Jersey therefore provided **(10)** ... testimony for a little-known period. After the end of its **(11)** ... , perhaps around 50,000 BC, the continuing presence of man in Jersey was **(12)** ... by only a few scattered finds of stone tools.

As the Ice Age glaciers **(13)** ... , the face of Europe changed. In the new dense forests, man exploited vast **(14)** ... of game, supplemented along **(15)** ... and rivers by rich harvests of fish and shellfish. This, the Middle Stone Age, seems to be a blank period for the Channel Islands, although some flintwork might be of this date.

0	**A** distinguished	**B** detached	**C** distinctive	**D** divided
1	**A** interest	**B** material	**C** observation	**D** type
2	**A** opened	**B** revealed	**C** sighted	**D** cleared
3	**A** hiding	**B** jumping	**C** covering	**D** including
4	**A** belonging	**B** open	**C** closed	**D** connected
5	**A** territory	**B** field	**C** scope	**D** grounds
6	**A** useful	**B** important	**C** helpful	**D** wealthy
7	**A** make	**B** produce	**C** provide	**D** control
8	**A** chase	**B** hunt	**C** tracking	**D** pursuit
9	**A** identified	**B** prepared	**C** transported	**D** developed
10	**A** unique	**B** grand	**C** entire	**D** fair
11	**A** reservation	**B** occupation	**C** residence	**D** observance
12	**A** concluded	**B** detached	**C** indicated	**D** exposed
13	**A** exhausted	**B** retired	**C** expired	**D** retreated
14	**A** resources	**B** stores	**C** varieties	**D** species
15	**A** beaches	**B** seas	**C** coasts	**D** lakes

Do not forget to put your answers on the answer sheet.

Example:

0	C		0
			▭ ▭

2   *For questions **16–30**, complete the following article by writing each missing word on the answer sheet.* **Use only one word for each space.** *The exercise begins with an example **(0)**.*

THE VEGETARIAN MEAL

Where vegetarian meals are served **(0)** ... courses, the parts **(16)** ... usually fitted into a relentless, unchanging pattern: soup, main course, salad, dessert. The first thing to do **(17)** ... considering the vegetarian cuisine **(18)** ... to get free of these stereotyped ideas. **(19)** ... , you may find yourself falling into **(20)** ... trap of 'substitutions'. Many vegetarian cookbooks have done **(21)** ... , imposing the old structure on to the vegetarian diet and trying to find 'meat substitutes'.

Vegetarian cookery is not a **(22)** ... for anything. It is a rich and various cuisine, full of many marvellous dishes **(23)** ... definite characteristics not in imitation of anything **(24)** ... – certainly not in imitation of meat. The vegetarian menu lends **(25)** ... to many arrangements. It need **(26)** ... be the slave of the 'main course', even though it does not avoid **(27)** ... arrangement when **(28)** ... seems fitting and useful. It **(29)** ... also consist of several equally important courses, **(30)** ... several dishes served at once.

Do not forget to put your answers on the answer sheet.

Example:

0	in	0
		▢ ▢

SECTION B

3 *In **most** lines of the following text, there is **one** spelling error. For each numbered line **31–44**, write the correctly spelled word in the spaces on your answer sheet. Some lines are correct. Indicate these lines with a tick (✓). The exercise begins with two examples (0).*

THE UNCERTAINTY OF SCIENCE

0	Science no longer holds any absolute truths. Even the
0	disciplin of physics, whose laws once went unchallenged,
31	has had to submit to the indignity of an Uncertainty Principale
32	In this climate of disbelief, we have begun to doubt even
33	fundamental propositions, and the old distintion between
34	natural and supernatural has become meaningless.
35	I find this tremendously exiting. The picture of science
36	as a jigsaw puzzle, with a finite number of peaces that would
37	one day all be slotted neatly into place, has never been
38	appealing. Experiance indicates that things are not like that
39	at all. Every new developement in the microscope reveals
40	farther minute detail in structures once thought to be
41	indivisable. Each enlargement in the power of the telescope
42	adds thousands of galaxies to a list allready so long that it is
43	meaningless to all but mathematicians. Even researche into what
44	once seemed to be simple behavour patterns has a way of going
	on forever.

Do not forget to put your answers on the answer sheet.

Example:

0	✓		0	▢ ▢
0	**discipline**		0	▢ ▢

4 For questions **45–58**, read the following note about an attendance certificate and use the information to complete the numbered gaps in the formal notice. Then write the new words in the correct spaces on your answer sheet. **Use no more than two words** for each gap. The exercise begins with an example (**0**). The words you need **do not occur** in the informal note.

INFORMAL NOTE

> *Dear Miki,*
> *How's the leg? I thought I'd better let you know what you have to do to get an attendance certificate from college. First, you must let the office know by next Monday if you want one. They don't hand them out automatically, because you have to go to all your classes (except the optional ones, of course), and be on time, and you have to do all your homework properly. If for some special reason, you haven't been able to do all this, but your Tutor is willing to say you deserve to get a certificate anyway, you must write and explain what was special about your situation. I'm sure they'll understand in your case. Let me know if I can do anything else.*
>
> *All the best, Jan*

FORMAL NOTICE

> ### CERTIFICATES OF ATTENDANCE
>
> Students (0) ... to receive certificates of attendance (45) ... the college office not (46) ... next Monday. Such certificates are issued (47) ... to those students who have (48) ... the college authorities with (49) ... to the (50) ... matters:
> * regular and (51) ... attendance at all (52) ... classes
> * satisfactory (53) ... of homework assignments
> Unless these (54) ... have been met in (55) ... , no certificate will be issued without a (56) ... explanation of exceptional (57) ... from the individual concerned in addition to the (58) ... of the tutor.

Do not forget to put your answers on the answer sheet.

Example:

0	wishing	0

SECTION C

5 *For questions* **59–65,** *read through the following text and then choose from list* **A–K** *the best phrase or sentence given below it to fill each of the blanks. Write one letter* **(A–K)** *in the correct box on your answer sheet. Some of the suggested answers do not fit at all. One answer has been given as an example* **(0).**

LANGUAGE AND SOCIETY

The most difficult task confronting us, in any period when there is a marked shift of social power, is the complicated process of revaluation of the inherited tradition. The common language, because in itself it is so crucial to this matter, **(0)** ... . It is clearly of vital importance to a culture that its common language **(59)** ... ; that it should, further, be adequate **(60)** ... , and to clarify change. **(61)** ... like English is still evolving, and great harm can be done to it by the imposition of crude categories of class. It is obvious that **(62)** ... , in the nineteenth century, of the new definition of 'standard English', particular uses of the common language have been taken and abused for the purposes of class distinction. Yet the dialect which is normally equated with standard English **(63)** ... . Some of its grammatical elements have a common importance, but not all of them. On the other hand, certain selected sounds have been given an authority **(64)** ... but simply from the fact that they are habitually made by persons who, for other reasons, **(65)** ... .

A But a language

B English grammar

C has no necessary superiority over other dialects

D since the development

E are of little or no importance

F provides an excellent instance

G should not decline in strength, richness and flexibility

H Whatever we may feel

I possess social and economic influence

J to express new experience

K which derives from no known law of language

Do not forget to put your answers on the answer sheet.

Example:

0	F		0
			▭ ▭

6 *Use the following notes to write instructions for visitors to a holiday cottage. Write* **one complete sentence** *on the answer sheet for each numbered set of notes, using connecting words and phrases as appropriate. You may add words and change the form of the words given in the notes but do not add any extra information. The first point has been expanded for you as an example* **(0).**

Ocean Ridge Cottage

0   Keys available from Mr Boyce, contact at Lazy Cat Cafe

81   Hire car booked (Bristows, garage opposite station) deposit (£25) payable on collection

82   From Bristows: left (Station Rd), follow Coast Road (clearly signed) 3 km, Ocean Ridge cottage top of hill

83   Water already connected, electricity meter behind door (£1 coins)

84   Phone – incoming calls only – in hall

85   NB path from back door to beach very steep, supervise children, cottage owner not responsible accidents

86   Lock cottage when out, unfortunately frequent theft from holiday homes recently – cash, credit cards, cameras etc.

The space below can be used for your rough answers.
Do not forget to put your answers on the answer sheet.

---

0   The keys are available from Mr Boyce, who can be contacted at the Lazy Cat Cafe.

81

82

83

84

85

86

PAPER 4 LISTENING (45 minutes)

Answer all questions.

SECTION A

You will hear a museum guide welcoming a party of visitors. Look at the notes below and complete the information for questions 1–8 using up to three words in each space.

You will hear the recording twice.

Lampley and District Museum

Section One – portraits of [_____ **1**] local people

– display illustrating local aspects of
[_____ **2**] events

Section Two – display related to Lampley's [_____ **3**]

– reconstruction of Lampley during [_____ **4**]

Section Three– models of [_____ **5**]

– pictures of [_____ **6**]

Section Four – audio-visual show called [_____ **7**]

– exhibition of [_____ **8**] by local artists

SECTION B

You will hear a recording from the telephone answering machine of a conference organiser. As you listen, fill in the information on the booking forms for questions 9–16.

Listen very carefully as you will hear this piece only ONCE.

International Conference Centre, Basing

Booking Form (Closed sessions)

Organisation: [   ] **9**

Contact name: [   ] **10**

Options: [   ] **11**

[   ] **12**

International Conference Centre, Basing

Booking Form (Closed sessions)

Organisation: [   ] **13**

Contact name: [   ] **14**

Options: [   ] **15**

[   ] **16**

SECTION C

*You will hear a radio programme in which a mother, Jane, and a father, Kenneth, discuss whether it is a good idea for young people to take a year out before going to university to travel around the world. During their discussion they express various views. For questions **17–24**, indicate which views are expressed by Jane and Kenneth, by writing J (for Jane)*
or K (for Kenneth)
or N (for neither) in the box provided.

You may write both initials if Jane and Kenneth express the same opinion.

You will hear the piece twice.

It's an opportunity to see the world with an open mind. ⬚ **17**

It's a good way to make new friends. ⬚ **18**

There's always a safe place to come home to. ⬚ **19**

Having travelled will be an advantage in their careers. ⬚ **20**

Living rough might expose them to disease. ⬚ **21**

It will be expensive. ⬚ **22**

They delay their start up the career ladder. ⬚ **23**

They'll learn to use their common sense. ⬚ **24**

You will hear extracts of five different people talking. They are all talking about some kind of meeting.

Task one

*Letters **A–H** list various different people. As you listen, put them in order by completing the boxes numbered **25–29** with the appropriate letter.*

Task two

*Letters **A–H** list the different meetings mentioned by the people speaking in the extracts. As you listen, put them in order by completing the boxes numbered **30–34** with the appropriate letter.*

You will hear the series twice.

Task one

A a mother	25
B a businessman	26
C a doctor	27
D a secretary	
E a rock star	28
F an old schoolfriend	29
G a local government official	
H a journalist	

Task two

A a successful negotiation	30
B a meeting that had previously been postponed	31
C a chance meeting	32
D breaking a friendship	33
E making new contacts	34
F finding unknown relatives	
G a missed meeting	
H a disappointing meeting	

Note: For Paper 5 see pages 144–147 and the Colour Section

Practice Test 2

PAPER 1 READING (1 hour 15 minutes)

Answer all questions.

FIRST TEXT / QUESTIONS 1–13

Answer questions **1–13** *by referring to the magazine article on pages 42–43.*

For questions **1–13** match the men with the opinions **A–J**. Some of the opinions may have been expressed by more than one of the men.
Note: Where one man has several opinions, these can be given **in any order**.

Bert Rogers   **1** ....   **2** ....   **3** ....

Howard Rogers   **4** ....   **5** ....

Jim Redmond   **6** ....   **7** ....

Derek Redmond   **8** ....   **9** ....   **10** ....

Roy Ackerman   **11** ....

Marcus Ackerman   **12** ....   **13** ....

Fathers:

A I encouraged my son to develop a particular ability.
B I don't agree with some of his political opinions.
C My son is not interested in my sort of work, although he's tried it.
D I think my son has been luckier than me.
E My son is similar to me in temperament.

Sons:

F I had no clear ambition when I was at school.
G I can confide in my father.
H I admire my father's abilities.
I My father and I are similar in character.
J I've only become close to my father since I've been an adult.

Fathers and Sons

BERT AND HOWARD ROGERS

Bert Rogers, 75, was production manager of a clothing factory before he retired. He has two sons. His younger son, Howard, 46, is an artist; he is married and has two small daughters.

BERT: "I missed out on quite a big part of Howard's childhood. When he was little I was working very long hours. I had to be content with seeing my children at weekends. We used to have outings to the seaside and the country, and visit museums and the sights in London.

"From an early age he was always working with paints and pencils. He had a natural talent for it – all I needed to do was guide and encourage him. I taught him the rules of perspective. We used to draw together because I, too, had always enjoyed painting and drawing.

"By the time he was 13, Howard had made up his mind that he wanted to be an artist. I would have preferred him to have followed a more academic career, but he left school at 16 and went to art college; I was disappointed, but I had no choice but to support him and try to take pride in his achievements.

"Even now, we still argue. Howard is quite fiery and volatile; temperamentally, he's far more like his mother than he is like me. He has quite strong left-wing views and we often clash. When we're arguing he gets quite emotional, but I respect him for his views, even though I think he's often wrong.

"Despite all this, I feel we're close; we can talk to each other and there is a considerable amount of affection between us, even though we may not always show it. Howard is a lovely chap; he's intelligent, gets on well with people and has a marvellous sense of humour.

"As an artist and a man who's expressing himself, he's on top of things. In a way, I envy him because he was able to do what he wanted to do. I'd hoped to train as an engraver, but my father wouldn't support my apprenticeship. I suppose because my own talent was wasted I made a point of encouraging Howard's, and I think it has been well worthwhile."

HOWARD: "My childhood memories of my father are pretty vague. Dad was a rather hazy comforting figure. He wasn't a powerful presence because he wasn't at home much. It's only now that I'm a father myself that I can understand what sort of person he is. He's kind and very understanding. I can talk to him more openly than I've ever done. We still row, but that's just part of our make-up, not because of any resentment.

"Since my children were born, I've seen much more of Dad than I used to. I love to see the pleasure he gets from them. The children have bridged some of the gap between us.

"Despite all the difficulties we've had in the past, I do love my father very much, and I think it's only quite recently that I've realised this.

"In many ways I feel sad for my father because I think many of his ambitions in life have been thwarted. I know, for example, that he wanted to become a gold engraver and his father wouldn't let him."

JIM AND DEREK REDMOND

Jim Redmond, 53, and son Derek, 27, made the headlines when runner Derek pulled a hamstring in the 400 m. semi-finals of the Barcelona Olympics. The photograph of father and son locked in an embrace was a memorable image of the Games.

JIM: "Derek was an active little boy, a bit of a handful. I enjoyed him very much when he was small, and I still do; in fact, we're pretty pally. When I was young I was away quite a lot, and got home late in the evenings. There are fathers who saw more of their sons, but I don't think it affected us badly.

"Derek was about six when I realised he was serious about sport and had potential. At first I was involved in his coaching as I had run at competitive levels many years ago. I didn't push him, though – only gave encouragement when I felt it necessary.

"After he left school, Derek worked in my company which supplies machinery for making meat products, but his heart wasn't in it.

"Derek and I are pretty close, we can talk about most subjects and our views are similar. I don't think he is always as thorough in some areas as I am, though. He is very good-natured and tends to give others the benefit of the doubt.

"When he was injured at the Olympics, it was the end of the Games for me. I hope all his hard work pays off and that he finally gets the medal he so richly deserves. He's a great person and I'm delighted with the way he's turned out."

DEREK: "My dad has followed my career since I was seven. He used to run when he was younger, so he had an interest. He could be tough in that he spelled out that I had to stick to what I'd chosen to do if I wanted to be good, but he never pushed me.

"Dad took an active part in my training until I was 12 and needed an experienced coach. Even now, we sit down and watch races together, then talk them over.

"When I was at school, Dad was a rep, and in the holidays I'd go out with him on calls. We used to talk about anything and everything; we were real mates, more than just father and son. And today, I can discuss anything about my professional or emotional life with Dad.

"When he started his business, I realised he has incredible drive – that's one of the things I admire most about him. He's very determined and will persevere until he gets what he wants. I think I share some of these qualities, but I can switch off more easily than he can.

I've got all the time in the world for my Dad."

ROY AND MARCUS ACKERMAN

Roy Ackerman, 50, is the Chairman of Leading Guides, which publishes the Egon Ronay and Ackerman Guides. He has recently made a six-part television series on cookery. Marcus, 23, has a flat next door to his father's Chelsea home.

ROY: "I see much more of Marcus now than when he was small. He's always popping in, and we have a meal together at least once a week. When Marcus was a child I was working as development director of a London food company and also running my own restaurants in Oxford. Although I wasn't aware of it at the time, I didn't spend as much time with him as I would have liked. I took him to museums and exhibitions, and our trip always included a good lunch or dinner – Marcus was into food at an early age!

"When he was a teenager I worried about Marcus's future. After he left school he did a number of different things including training in the catering and hotel industry, and working as a fitness instructor.

"Eventually, he did come to work for me as an assistant in the publishing office. I think I was quite tough on him, probably far tougher than I'd dare to be with anyone else. At the moment he's working in retailing, to get some experience of that side of business life.

"Overall, Marcus and I get on pretty well. If we have arguments it's usually because one of us is tired or irritable. Neither of us bear grudges, though, so we always make up with a phone call shortly

after.

"We are alike in quite a few ways – we're both good at thinking up ideas and putting things together, but sometimes not as good at the following-through part. I'll often discuss business plans with him to get his views on things, even if I don't always follow his suggestions.

"I'm proud of Marcus in many ways. He's a very sociable person and great company. He relates well to people of all ages and always seems to make a good impression."

MARCUS: "I think as families go, we're pretty close. One of my earliest memories of Roy is waking up one morning – it must have been a birthday – to find he'd put up a load of scaffolding for a surprise play area in the garden. I also remember being around the restaurants as a child, poking my fingers in things, and being chased out by the chefs – it was a kid's paradise.

"Occasionally as a child I did feel a bit neglected; Roy worked such long hours. I wasn't terribly happy at school and was glad to leave at 16. I didn't want to go to college, but wasn't sure what I *did* want to do. My ideas for the future are getting clearer. I think eventually I'd like to have my own restaurant or club.

"When I was working for Roy, it did sometimes annoy me to be constantly at his beck and call. I'll never have his incredible drive. He left home at 14 to make his own way in the world. I haven't had to struggle as he did.

"Roy has taught me a great deal. He is a real 'people' person – comfortable in any situation. He also impresses me with the amount of information he is able to absorb and store. I'm very aware of the fact that having Roy as a father has smoothed the path for me. I've had lots of opportunities because of him."

Remember to put your answers on the separate answer sheet.

930
945.

SECOND TEXT / QUESTIONS 14–18

Read the following magazine article by William Boyd and answer questions 14–18.

Bookshop Readings

I can remember the first reading I attended, a long time ago. It wasn't even in a bookshop. At the venue – some hall, some large dusty room – we filed in and took our seats. I was oddly apprehensive, and it wasn't just because of the oppressive, humid warmth of the room, the big windows hot with summer evening sun; it wasn't either the usual tense geniality disguising the edginess that arises when too many writers, or would-be writers, find themselves in the same place at the same time. No, it was something to do with the very occasion itself. This "reading" lark – it didn't feel right, it was strange and unsettling.

The author sidled self-consciously up to the lectern, then, in a monotone of surpassing dullness, he announced that, in an ideal world, he would have read the entire novel to us this evening but that tonight (nervous stirrings in the audience), for regrettable but obvious reasons of time, he would have to restrict himself to a mere three or four chapters.

We got through it: time slowed to a torpid, snail-like crawl. Subjective aeons passed before we were released to the pleasures of the buffet.

And all the while I kept saying to myself: what are we doing here? Why do we subject ourselves to this ordeal? This is not *natural*. It will never catch on.

How things have changed. And I admit my reservations were wrong-headed. True, the essential act of reading is still that silent, intimate encounter between writer and reader, as the text unspools in the reader's mind, but the evidence is overwhelming: I have to recognise that there are ancillary, audible pleasures to be had also. People like to *hear* a writer read.

"Read" is the key word, too. I assumed readings became popular because of some sneaking curiosity about the writer, a desire to check the original out against the air-brushed, retouched, fetchingly shadowed photo on the bookjacket. To hear the voice, to see the clothes, to scrutinise the flawed and blinking face gives the reader a momentary frisson of what? Power? Reassurance? Clandestine hilarity? I could understand those motives, I thought. I know *you*, the

reader thinks as the author rises to his or her feet, but you don't know me.

But again, I think I'm on the wrong track. Those needs are satisfied in a second or two, so there must be other factors at stake. Sometimes, remembering my own stupefied boredom at readings, I offer to talk rather than read, assuming that some free-associating reflections on "being a writer" are bound to be more diverting, but I am invariably politely turned down. "People want to hear writers read" is the constant response.

Indeed they do, and to such an extent that we now have an ever-growing circuit, a veritable expanding tour available. Like those minor rock bands in their minibuses moving from university student union to pub to village hall, writers criss-cross the country from bookshop to bookshop, reading from their new novels, story collections, their biographies or whatever. Sometimes dashingly solo, sometimes grouped under catch-all categories ("four Liverpudlian travel writers read from their work in progress"), sometimes celebrating notional anniversaries (Best of Young British Revisited) or new imprints, on any given night in a bookshop, you will find an author or two undergoing a now familiar *rite*.

The diffident arrival, then the calming drink. Then all those strangers waiting to listen to your voice. Then the relief of the question-and-answer session, the grateful signing of bought copies. Writers now reminisce and anecdotalise like members of touring theatre companies, swopping information on the good and bad gigs, speculating on the generosity of this manager as opposed to the parsimony of that. Without really being aware of it, we have witnessed a small revolution taking place. The performance side of a writer's life – which 10 years ago was almost non-existent – now dominates the publication of a book to a remarkable degree. Perhaps there is an atavistic undercurrent to the encounter between reader and writer. After all, it was the storyteller who used to hunker down around the campfire with the other members of the tribe and who had to tell a tale that would fascinate and enthral for an hour or so. Today, canapé in trembling hand, microphone at the ready, the writer is fulfilling a similar role – as well as trying to flog as many books as possible. If it goes wrong, all sorts of uncertainties intrude, and never has the lonely security of the ivory tower seemed more appealing. And when it goes well, other more heady temptations accumulate. The reading is a kind of test, and perhaps here is the key to its sly addiction.

The public encounter forcibly reminds us of our origins as story tellers and of the responsibilities – to intrigue, to beguile, to entertain – that the role demands. Here the currency that underpins the tacit contract between writer and reader is on open display, and in front of an audience its quality – or otherwise – can all too easily be discerned.

---

14 How did William Boyd feel about the first reading he attended?

   A It was a waste of money.
   B The audience was too big.
   C The audience could not understand the work being read.
   D Such events would not become widely popular.

15 Why does he believe people go to readings?

   A They want the opportunity to meet someone well-known.
   B It gives them a feeling of superiority.
   C It's more fulfilling than reading for oneself.
   D They enjoy hearing the words in the author's own voice.

16 How has the significance of readings altered in recent years?

   A They have become an important part of the publishing scene.
   B There are now too many of them.
   C They have become too much like other forms of entertainment.
   D They are a useful way for authors to get together.

17 How does the modern author at a reading differ from traditional storytellers?

   A He is more likely to be nervous.
   B There is competition from other forms of entertainment.
   C He has a commercial purpose for what he is doing.
   D His audience is more critical.

18 What makes writers continue to give readings?

   A Writing is a lonely profession.
   B It's a good way to assess one's work.
   C It pays well.
   D They enjoy meeting their fans.

Remember to put your answers on the separate answer sheet.

THIRD TEXT / QUESTIONS 19–25

Read this magazine article, then choose the best paragraph from **A–H** *to fill each gap* **19–25**. *There is one extra paragraph which does not belong in any of the gaps.*

Kellogg's story

In the modern world, there is great awareness of the value of balanced diets.

19	

The brothers were Dr John Harvey Kellogg, the Superintendent of Battle Creek Sanatarium in Battle Creek, Michigan, USA, and his younger brother – Will Keith.

20	

As pioneers in linking diet to disease prevention and the maintenance of good health, the Kellogg brothers spent a lot of time trying to develop cereal foods, which would be both nutritious and palatable for patients – whilst providing fibre and carbohydrates, and reducing fat intake!

21	

In a series of recipe experiments, W.K. and J.H. Kellogg ran boiled wheat dough through rollers to produce thin sheets of wheat, which they toasted and ground into meal. In this quest for healthier food, the brothers continued to experiment with grains, which they were convinced held the key to better health.

22	

An interruption in their activities led to a batch of cooked wheat being left in the lab for more than a day. It was decided to proceed with the batch anyway and when the wheat ran through rollers, they were delighted to discover the rollers discharged flakes instead of the customary sheet of wheat. The extra time between cooking and rolling made all the difference.

23	

As a result, the Kellogg brothers started a food manufacturing company separate from the sanatarium, and the ready-to-eat cereal food was born! In 1906 W.K. Kellogg formed his own company – the Battle Creek Toasted Corn Flake Company – now known the world over as "Kellogg's".

24	

In 1923, Kellogg's became one of the first companies to employ a full time nutritionist, Mary Barber, with the aim of producing and standardising recipes, as well as assisting schools, communicators and consumers with information on nutrition.

25	

The Kellogg brothers would be proud that the Kellogg Company of today places such importance on the nutritious value of the food it produces. It is also no coincidence that current Kellogg cereals fit so well with recommendations that are made by the Department of Health – a tribute to those Kellogg pioneers at the turn of the century.

A Modern dietary recommendations urge us to eat more dietary fibre and carbohydrates ... and to consume less fat. These guidelines may be new to many of us, but, in fact, they formed the cornerstone of the philosophy of the Kellogg brothers – back at the turn of the century!

B The advantage of a cereal breakfast goes further than this. Remember that dietary guidelines relate to your diet as a whole. So, if you start the day in credit with a cereal breakfast you can afford a few high-fat treats later in the day without exceeding your fat target.

C The following year the British company was formed, with Corn Flakes and All-Bran initially imported from Canada. In 1938, Britain's first Kellogg factory was opened in Manchester.

D The tasty product, later to be known as Corn Flakes, quickly became popular among patients and many requested a supply of the food after returning home.

E The duo were well ahead of their time, and their endeavours in the quest for healthier foods led them to the discovery and development of breakfast cereals.

F In the following decades, the company expanded around the world, providing cereals which were not only healthy, but highly enjoyable. The emphasis on nutritious value, which was part of the Kellogg philosophy, was always maintained during the years of growth.

G The sanatarium was internationally famous at the time, and offered patients exercise, fresh air and a strict diet which prohibited caffeine, alcohol, tobacco and meat.

H In 1884, the brothers discovered the secret to making a flaked cereal, an idea they had been working on for some time.

Remember to put your answers on the separate answer sheet.

10 ^10
10 25 -

FOURTH TEXT / QUESTIONS 26–40

Answer questions 26–40 by referring to the newspaper article on pages 49–50.

For questions 26–40 match the names A–H with the statements about their life and work. Some of the names apply to more than one statement.

This writer/translator

has found a way to describe the workings of a dictatorship.	26 ....
has translated a translation.	27 ....
has sometimes had to ask the author to explain a meaning.	28 ....
suffered political oppression.	29 ....
believes good translators are bound to have difficulties in their work.	30 ....
was the child of immigrants.	31 ....
translates in his/her spare time.	32 ....
has known people whose lives resembled those in a book he/she has translated.	33 ....
lived abroad as a child.	34 ....
uses traditional expressions.	35 ....
has found that enjoying a book makes it easier to translate.	36 ....
believes it's important to translate meanings rather than words.	37 ....
believes that a translation should reflect the original language.	38 ....
makes up words which didn't previously exist.	39 ....
has worked as a language teacher.	40 ....

A	Pontiero
B	Saramago
C	Wilson
D	Klima
E	Lane
F	Goytisolo
G	Bray
H	Kadare

TRANSLATORS

Comfortable at sea in syntax

Sabine Durrant talks to Helen Lane, translator of *Makbara* by Juan Goytisolo (Serpent's Tail, £9.99)

WITH Helen Lane, we're talking figures. She is 72. Over the last 50 years, she has translated 85 books. She speaks five languages (English, French, Italian, Spanish and Portuguese). She has received a total of 20 grants from three Ministries of Culture. She has won three major prizes for translation in her native United States – two of them twice. And is she smug? "Everybody comes into the world to find what they do best," she says humbly from her home in the Dordogne. "What I do best happens to be translation. It's my contribution for having lived."

Experience has not brought with it conservatism. Lane considers herself to be an "avant-garde" translator, which means that whereas other translators may pride themselves on creating something that reads as if it was always written in English, she prefers to "make the syntax a little strange to remind readers that they're reading a translation". It also means that she's most comfortable when at sea in the syntax of the Spanish writer Juan Goytisolo. She has collaborated on all his works, and it doesn't get any easier.

Occasionally, she would despair over a word and, after hurling her eight Spanish dictionaries into a corner, ring Goytisolo at his home in Paris. "Usually," she says, with 50 years' experience in her voice, "it would turn out to be a word he'd invented."

Messages transmitted by facts

Peter Guttridge talks to Paul Wilson, translator of *My Golden Trades* by Ivan Klima (Granta, £13.99)

IN THE 10 years Toronto-based translator Paul Wilson spent in Czechoslovakia, he saw many friends put in the same position as the one Ivan Klima describes in *My Golden Trades*, the most autobiographical of all the author's works. Klima, who in recent years has begun to achieve the recognition he deserves as a writer and thinker, was prevented in the 1980s from publishing his books by the authorities and so had to take a variety of jobs – "golden trades" – to earn a living. "The atmosphere was very familiar to me," Wilson says.

Wilson, who abandoned an MA at London University on George Orwell in 1967 to teach English in Czechoslovakia, began translating essays and articles soon after he moved to Prague. However, his first substantial piece of work – the English translation of Josef Skvorecky's *magnum opus The Engineer of Human Souls* – came after Skvorecky was expelled in 1977 (he went to Canada). Since then he has translated novels and essays by many writers, notably Vaclav Havel. "*My Golden Trades* is one of the easiest books I have translated because I was so delighted with the text," Wilson says. "There is a sense of celebration about the book because the pieces were written either when things were easing in Czechoslovakia or when freedom had come."

Sorcerer in the national night

Nick Caistor talks to Barbara Bray, translator of *The Palace of Dreams* by Ismail Kadare (Harvill, £7.99)

"ISMAIL KADARE writes in a minority language about a hidden culture: Albania," says his translator Barbara Bray. "To get his message out he has to be something of a witch, a sorcerer." Bray herself, working from the French version of *The Palace of Dreams* without reference to the original Albanian edition, describes her own task in similar terms when she speaks of the obligation to explore beyond the ambiguities of the words on the page and "enter into a kind of trance to work out what the author was really driving at".

The Palace of Dreams is a parable about the way in which an all-pervasive oppressive state collects and interprets the dreams of its subjects, invading even the subconscious life of the nation. Bray saw as one of the basic intentions of the book the suggestion that language and meaning are slippery and elusive, and how easy it is to corrupt people by manipulating language.

"The translator is in a privileged position in this respect," Bray insists. "So many people think there is a direct equivalence between language and thought, but the translator knows the traps that language can set for you, the way it both leads and misleads."

This awareness is what matters for Bray, who has translated widely from French authors: the struggle to tease meaning from the text.

In this sense, she frankly admits, "the author can get in the way sometimes". She has no hesitation in speaking of the translator's efforts as a "mission", aimed first and foremost at upholding "the integrity of one's own language". What is shared with the original author, however, is the passionately felt conviction that "language is a mystery which can be pierced".

Adventures in humility

Robert Winder talks to Giovanni Pontiero, who translated *The Year of the Death of Ricardo Reis* by José Saramago (Harvill, £14.99)

THE MOST striking and unex-pected thing about Giovanni Pontiero is his dry Glaswegian accent. His parents were Italian, but he was born in Scotland; he spent two years in Brazil, but is now a professor at Manchester University. "I suppose you could say I'm a bit of a mongrel," he says.

"I couldn't say what my first language is. Truth is, I'm probably most at home in Brazilian Portuguese. But it's not so much a question of being interested in language as of being *worried* by language. Saramago once said that the only translators who worried him were the ones who didn't have any problems."

Pontiero has translated many works by the Brazilian writer Clarice Lispector, and now he is as thoroughly engaged by the Portuguese novelist José Saramago: *The Year of the Death of Ricardo Reis* is his second work to appear in English.

He is modest about the translator's role, and uses the word "humility" frequently. But in Saramago's case, fidelity was not a straightforward matter. "He's very fond of aphorisms and proverbs – there's almost a history of popular culture in there. But our proverbs don't quite match, they sound either dated or too modern."

For Pontiero there is a gratifying cross-over between his life as an academic and his work as a translator. He hopes, in the future, to write biographies of both Lispector and Saramago. But it leaves little room for manoeuvre. "I get up at 5.30 as a rule and try to do three and a half hours before I go to the university. I love explaining to students what it is that makes this work great. And the academic side of me loves the research. With Saramago every book is so totally new."

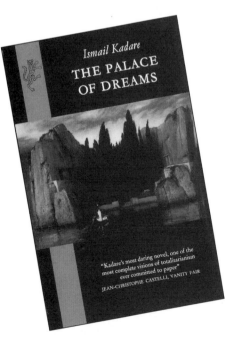

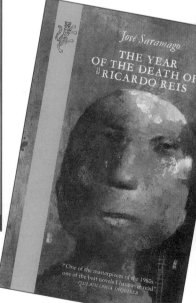

PAPER 2 WRITING (2 hours)

This paper contains one Section A task and four Section B tasks. You must complete the Section A task and one task from Section B.

1 While studying in England, you become involved with a local charity which supports homeless people in the area where you live. Part of your work is to help Paul Enfield, the Project Manager, with the correspondence. **Using the information provided**, write the letter and notice listed below.

WINTER WARMTH for the homeless

Do you have a little time to spare?

Information sheet for volunteer applicants

Who are we?

Winter Warmth is a locally based charity which provides services for homeless people. It was founded in 1990 and has since then provided nightshelter and food for the many homeless people in this area.

What might you do?

THE DROP-IN PROJECT

At the Drop-in-centre based at the former Corner House Café in Clifton Street, you will help provide food and drink at very low cost. You'll also offer information and advice for people who are suffering the stress of homelessness and isolation. You will be a member of a team of three, working under your Team Leader, and you'll probably do this once a fortnight. The Project Manager (or Deputy) will be on site every evening to offer support to you and your customers.

THE NIGHTSHELTER

At the moment we are still in the planning stage, but we hope to open this year's shelter at the end of November. We are, however, recruiting volunteers early so that full training can be given. We aim to provide a safe space for people to sleep overnight through the winter months. A paid worker will be on site at all times to offer support and deal with any difficulties. As a volunteer, you will be asked to work one overnight or one early morning shift per fortnight to set up bedding, serve drinks and talk with customers or to serve breakfast and clear away the bedding.

THE CENTRAL SERVICES UNIT

Could you lend a hand with the administration of Winter Warmth? If you have skills in word processing, desk-top publishing, book-keeping, fund-raising or general admin, we'd love to hear from you. We need people who can offer a couple of regular hours each week or who can offer consultancy on an occasional basis.

Anyone wishing to offer their services as a volunteer is asked to contact

Winter Warmth
101, Green Street
Oakstead OK2 4JH
Phone 672413

Winter Warmth is a registered charity
Reg no 10040300

HOWLETT MOTORS (Oakstead) Ltd

25–31 High Street
Oakstead OK1 2AR
Tel: (0223) 56565
Fax: (0223) 57583

Robert J. Howlett
Director

Green Street,

Monday, Sept 20th

Hi!

We think we've found another source of funding.
Apparently, Howlett's Garage had a very good year last
year and old Bob Howlett is feeling generous. Do you
think you could draft a letter asking him for a
donation? Tell him what we do, and you could mention
about having all different sorts as volunteers,
housewives, students etc etc. Make sure we sound
really efficient — he won't give anything if he thinks
we waste money because of muddle. It's so important we
get more of these local business guys involved,
specially now the rent on the café's going up. Perhaps
you could bring the draft to next week's planning
meeting?

   Could you also write a notice to go out to committee
members & team leaders, giving time and place of the
meeting (Monday, 6.30, in this office) and an outline
agenda? That is, we'll be discussing your letter,
fund-raising in general & organising schedules. I'll
pick it up later and get it circulated.

Cheers!

Paul

PS Sheila says she heard he gave some money to the
children's hospital last year, so you might mention
him being known to be charitable or some such, just to
flatter him a bit. I attach his business card for the
address.

Now write

(a) **a letter** to Mr Howlett, asking him for financial support (about 200 words)

(b) **a notice** to be sent to committee members as requested by Paul (about 50 words)

You must set them out in an appropriate way.

SECTION B

*Choose **ONE** of the following writing tasks. Your answer should follow exactly the instructions given. You are advised to write approximately 250 words.*

2 You have been asked to write **a section of your local tourist guidebook** entitled 'Getting to know local people'. Your contribution should include suggestions for different age groups.

3 You have just received a letter from a young friend which includes the following paragraph:

> *Well, that's the end of college, and long vacations, and now I've got to get used to the idea of going out to work like everybody else! It's a bit daunting really. I know you've managed to make a success of your career and still find time to enjoy life. Would you like to give me any advice?*

Write **a letter of advice** to your friend.

4 A fellow student is doing research into children's perceptions of school. She is currently collecting information about children's reactions to starting at a new school. Write **an account** of your first few days at primary **or** secondary school, describing your experiences and your feelings.

5 You decide to apply for this job which you see advertised in a student newspaper. Write **a letter of application**.

Thinking of a career in travel and tourism?
Here's an ideal opportunity to find out all about it!

Caseway Travel

is looking for enthusiastic helpers in their busy information and booking office for two months this summer.

You will have plenty of chances to meet tourists from the UK and all over the world and to help them sort out accommodation, travel and sightseeing in the North of England, as well as assisting our travel clerks with international reservations and ticketing.

No formal qualifications are required, but you must speak good English and at least one other language. You will be someone who enjoys meeting all sorts of people, who keeps calm and smiles under pressure, and is quick to learn.

In return we offer a good weekly salary, pleasant working conditions and the possibility of turning a summer job into a permanent post if appropriate.

Write, giving full information about yourself, to:
J.P. Parker, Caseway Travel, Harbour Walk, Dunton, NB12 8LR, England

---

PAPER 3 ENGLISH IN USE (1 hour 30 minutes)

Answer all questions.

SECTION A

1 *For questions **1–15**, read the text below and decide which word on page 55 best fits each space. Put the letter you choose for each question in the correct box on your answer sheet. The exercise begins with an example* (**0**).

RENOIR THE FILM DIRECTOR

Film directors usually make the least promising subjects for biography. They **(0)** ... to stay behind the camera and get on with making films, emerging only to make the **(1)** ... promotional statement. Only rarely is a film-maker interesting enough to **(2)** ... biographical interest, and some pay off the attention handsomely. What biographer could **(3)** ... analysing Hitchcock, Woody Allen or Polanski? These directors, in any case, were themselves sufficiently absorbed in their own **(4)** ... to cross over to the other side of the camera and **(5)** ... themselves to the public.

Much of Jean Renoir's public profile is **(6)** ... on his appearance in his final film. But judging by the most recent biography, by Ronald Bergan, the man was simply not that interesting. He grew up in the benevolent **(7)** ... of his painter father, against whom he appears not to have **(8)** ... in any way, emerged to make his own **(9)** ... in the early French cinema, and went on making films for most of the rest of his life. Even when **(10)** ... by war, Renoir seems to have **(11)** ... through his career with equanimity, fuelled by the love of all around him.

It may be that there is nothing new to say about the director's life, since he dealt with it so thoroughly in two **(12)** ... . Bergan takes a lot from Renoir's accounts, although he does point out the occasional discrepancy between memory and **(13)** ... . The biography is too **(14)** ... to strike any life into the subject. Bergan's assessments of the films are level-headed and pay **(15)** ... attention to their formal achievement, but cast no new light on them.

0	**A** incline	**B** tend	**C** determine	**D** insist
1	**A** odd	**B** strange	**C** peculiar	**D** particular
2	**A** award	**B** prize	**C** value	**D** merit
3	**A** oppose	**B** resist	**C** confront	**D** expel
4	**A** view	**B** image	**C** trend	**D** expression
5	**A** display	**B** examine	**C** allow	**D** distinguish
6	**A** described	**B** based	**C** imagined	**D** gathered
7	**A** memory	**B** vision	**C** shadow	**D** regard
8	**A** rebelled	**B** related	**C** referred	**D** resisted
9	**A** spot	**B** field	**C** mark	**D** point
10	**A** faced	**B** tackled	**C** charged	**D** opposed
11	**A** flown	**B** sailed	**C** wandered	**D** run
12	**A** souvenirs	**B** memoirs	**C** revivals	**D** reminiscences
13	**A** idea	**B** account	**C** story	**D** fact
14	**A** inventive	**B** respectful	**C** inaccurate	**D** resourceful
15	**A** due	**B** right	**C** just	**D** fine

Do not forget to put your answers on the answer sheet.

Example:

0	B		0
			▢ ▢

2 *For questions* **16–30**, *complete the following text by writing each missing word on your answer sheet.* **Use only one word for each space**. *The exercise begins with an example* (**0**).

TOURING NORTH WALES

There is a wide variety of hotel accommodation in the beautiful city of Chester, which lies (**0**) ... over the border in England, making it the ideal starting-point (**16**) ... touring North Wales. (**17**) ... of the pleasures of travelling through Wales, (**18**) ... in the north or the south, (**19**) ... that the perceptive visitor will readily learn about (**20**) ... history, mythology and folklore of this lovely country. Probably no (**21**) ... part of Britain is peopled with so (**22**) ... lovers of music and poetry. The Welsh are people (**23**) ..., in the shops, the pubs and (**24**) ... the High Street, delight in discussing not only the arts (**25**) ... a wide variety of topics such as politics, religion and local history. Thus, in (**26**) ... remotest of Welsh villages, it is always possible to learn about history and traditions ranging (**27**) ... over centuries. For the tourist, numerous excellent hotels, guest houses and farmhouses that provide accommodation (**28**) ... to be found throughout North Wales. It is probably fair (**29**) ... say that prices in general tend to be lower than (**30**) ... charged in similar establishments in England.

Do not forget to put your answers on the answer sheet.

Example:

0	just		0
			▭ ▭

SECTION B

3 *In most lines of the following text, there is one word **which is not in the correct form**. For each numbered line **31–43**, write the correctly formed word in the space on your answer sheet. Some lines are correct. Indicate these lines with a tick (✓). The exercise begins with three examples (0).*

THE ENGLISH PLANT COLLECTORS

0	Who were the people responsible for collection and sending plants from one
0	country to another? And why did they do it? Initially they were travellers with
0	other purpose: traders, colonists, pilgrims and missionaries have all been
31	important in providing new plants for English gardens. They sent back
32	indigenous wild plants, or sometimes, as in the cases of visitors to China and
33	Japan, plants which have been cultivated and improved for hundreds of years.
34	This worked, of course, in both directions: English gardens were making in
	the most unlikely places.
35	Travellers did not always recognise an interesting plant on seen it – interesting,
36	that is, to the collector at home. So in the 16th and 17th century, attempts were
37	made to collect on a most professional basis, either by patrons sending
38	collections into the field, or by subscriptions to finance local enthusiasts in the
39	most promised areas. By 1611 John Tradescant was travelling and collecting
40	in France and other parts of Europe. Lately, Peter Collinson, a London
41	merchant, who had seen the richness of the plant material sending back by
42	Tradescant, organised a syndicate to finance the amateur botanical John
43	Bartram. Before long, special collectors were being dispatched to all parts of
	the world by institutions such as the Chelsea Physic Garden.

Do not forget to put your answers on the answer sheet.

Example:

0	collecting	0
0	✓	0
0	purposes	0

4 *For questions **44–55**, read the following note about the visit of a government minister to a college and use the information given to complete the gaps in the formal report. Then write the new words in the correct spaces on your answer sheet. **Use no more than two words** for each gap. The exercise begins with an example **(0)**. The words you need **do not occur** in the note.*

NOTE

> Dear James
>
> Sorry you missed the big day – but hope you had a good holiday! Anyway, it all went pretty smoothly, so the report won't take long to draft.
>
> He rolled up dead on time, and the Dean said his bit about how pleased we all were to see him and then took him along to his office for a bit of a private talk. After about half an hour they came out and a student took him to see some of the bits where students live. Then we all sat down to lunch, all done by the students, which he said really nice things about, better than the Ministry canteen, according to him! After lunch he spent a few minutes in a couple of classes, talked to a few students, asking what they were doing and so on. Then he popped into the library, saw the state of the roof, said he could see why we needed money, and that was it.
>
> I wasn't there when he left, but I gather he sounded as if he really means to try and get us some extra cash. The Dean says he's quite hopeful, anyway.
>
> See you soon. All the best.
> Margaret

FORMAL REPORT

> *VISIT TO WESTLAND COLLEGE BY THE MINISTER OF EDUCATION*
> The minister arrived **(0)** ... and was **(44)** ... by the Dean, Dr Jaffari. After some private **(45)** ... with the Dean, the Minister **(46)** ... some typical **(47)** ... by a student. Lunch **(48)** ... by students on the catering course. The minister **(49)** ... the food, which he **(50)** ... favourably to that served at the Ministry. Following lunch, the Minister **(51)** ... classes, where he met the students, and then the library, where **(52)** ... was drawn to the poor **(53)** ... of the roof. He agreed that there is clearly **(54)** ... for extra funding. The Dean feels that he has **(55)** ... to be optimistic about this.

Do not forget to put your answers on the answer sheet.

Example:

0	punctually	0

SECTION C

5 *For questions **56–61**, read through the following text and then choose from list **A–J** the best phrase or sentence given below it to fill each of the blanks. Write one letter **(A–J)** in the correct box on your answer sheet. **Some of the suggested answers do not fit at all.** One answer has been given as an example **(0)**.*

THE KURGAN

Six thousand years ago, the Kurgan emerged on the vast grasslands of the Eurasian steppes. They were the first people to breed horses that could carry human mounts, **(0)** ... . The Kurgan conquered the steppes, **(56)** ... . Their era marked the beginning of a journey of pastoral conquest **(57)** ... in the American west, the tropical forests of Central and South America and the arid plains of the Australian outback.

The Kurgan transformed Europe over a 3,000-year period of invasion and conquest but **(58)** ... , no works of art and no written records, their influence has largely been ignored by historians. And yet that influence has been great. **(59)** ... , security is found in a deep sense of belonging to the land. **(60)** ... had no such allegiance to place. Land was something to capture, possess and exploit. It had strategic and economic value, **(61)** ... .

A but no sacred or intrinsic value

B The nomadic Kurgans

C Under the Kurgan influence

D allowing them to manage large herds of cattle over vast regions

E creating the first great nomadic cattle empire in world history

F that could be used in trade with other cultures

G that continues today

H having left no physical monuments

I In agricultural societies

J lacking a common culture

Do not forget to put your answers on the answer sheet.

Example:

0	D		0

6   *A friend who is expecting a large number of visitors has asked you if you can help with suggestions for suitable food. Use the following notes and write him instructions for making a rice salad. Write* **one complete sentence** *on the answer sheet for each numbered set of notes, using connecting words and phrases as appropriate. You may add words and change the form of the words given in the notes but do not add any extra information. The first point has been expanded for you as an example* **(0)***.*

> **0**   Need recipes can prepare before visitors
> **81** Suggest rice salad – easy, tasty, not expensive
> **82** Ingredients: lots of colourful veg (small chunks), eg carrots, peppers + onion, rice & dressing
> **83** Use large, heavy pan: soften veg in oil/butter (5 mins)
> **84** Add water, rice, salt – cook → rice done
> **85** Make dressing: mix lemon juice/vinegar + oil (?olive), mustard & pepper
> **86** Rinse rice & veg (hot water), before cool → dressing, stir well
> **87** Also good: chopped nuts/eggs/cheese – add with dressing

The space below can be used for your rough answers.
Do not forget to put your answers on the answer sheet.

> Dear Pat,
> **0**   I know you need recipes for food you can prepare before your visitors arrive.
>
> **81**
>
> **82**
>
> **83**
>
> **84**
>
> **85**
>
> **86**
>
> **87**
>
> Good luck, and have a nice time with your visitors!
> Best wishes,

PAPER 4 LISTENING (45 minutes)

Answer all questions.

*Candy Watkins works in the tourist office of a small town in the west of England. Each morning her first job is to check the messages on the telephone answering machine for her boss, Heather. Look at her notes below and complete the information for questions **1–9**.*

You will hear the recording twice.

MEMO

Hensham Tourist Office

TO: Heather
FROM: Candy   July 15

Phone messages

Mr & Mrs Benkel, from [_____ **1**], want to book

three nights b & b at a [_____ **2**], starting Friday.

Will phone back to confirm.

Monty Durham, From Henmouth [_____ **3**] Office:

the [_____ **4**] are ready.

[_____ **5**] will deliver direct. How many do we need?

Oxbow Players summer show will be called [_____ **6**], a comedy.

Location: [_____ **7**]

Date: [_____ **8**]

Martin will come to office about [_____ **9**]

SECTION B

You will hear a college tutor giving some information to a group of students about arrangements for a field trip. As you listen, fill in the information on the booking form for questions 10–16.

Listen very carefully as you will hear this piece only ONCE.

FIELD TRIP

footwear must be [_____ **10**]

jacket must have [_____ **11**]

luggage – best sort is backpack with [_____ **12**]

food – bring some [_____ **13**]

don't bring [_____ **14**]

stationery – bring two [_____ **15**]

and a plastic [_____ **16**]

SECTION C

You will hear a discussion between three people, Ray, Nonna and Owen, who are talking about the problems they have in travelling around the city where they live. For questions 17–26, indicate which solutions are proposed by each speaker. Write R for Ray,
             or N for Nonna,
             or O for Owen, in the box provided.
You should write one initial only for each answer.

You will hear the piece twice.

cycle lanes beside roads [___ **17**]

cycle paths away from roads [___ **18**]

'park and ride' schemes [___ **19**]

free buses [___ **20**]

subsidised buses [___ **21**]

underground car parks [___ **22**]

high car parking charges [___ **23**]

pedestrianised city centre [___ **24**]

renewal of urban railway system [___ **25**]

underground railway system [___ **26**]

SECTION D

You will hear extracts of five different people talking. They are all talking about something to do with health.

Task one

*Letters **A–H** list various different people. As you listen, put them in order by completing the boxes numbered **27–31** with the appropriate letter.*

Task two

*Letters **A–H** list the purposes of the people speaking in the extracts. As you listen, put them in order by completing the boxes numbered **32–36** with the appropriate letter.*

You will hear the series twice.

Task one

A a parent

B a student

C a surgeon

D a social worker

E a doctor's receptionist

F an employer

G an employee

H a dentist

	27
	28
	29
	30
	31

Task two

A making an excuse

B cancelling an appointment

C explaining a proposed treatment

D asking advice

E showing off

F expressing sympathy

G suggesting a course of action

H offering financial help

	32
	33
	34
	35
	36

Note: For Paper 5 see pages 147–148 and the Colour Section.

Practice Test 3

PAPER 1 READING (1 hour 15 minutes)

Answer all questions.

FIRST TEXT / QUESTIONS 1–14

Answer questions **1–14** by referring to the book reviews on pages 65–66.

For questions **1–14**, match each of the statements below to one of the book reviews **A–J**. Some of the reviews apply to more than one of the statements.

The book is

an academic study of one kind of habitat.   **1** ....

a guide for those who have recently become interested in studying the environment.   **2** ....

a guide book for walkers.   **3** ....

known to have upset some scientists.   **4** ....

concerned with the need for us to know more about the variety of species on Earth.   **5** ....

arguing that some large-scale projects may be foolish undertakings.   **6** ....

about a species which is well-known but widely misunderstood.   **7** ....

a description of a theory about how the Earth functions.   **8** ....

an influential account of environmental damage.   **9** ....

an emotive account of one species.   **10** ....

written in the style of a different type of book.   **11** ....

suggesting that action is necessary to prevent disaster.   **12** ....

an account of a research project.   **13** ....

a beautifully-written work by an exceptional character.   **14** ....

Remember to put your answers on the separate answer sheet.

Book Reviews

A

After ploughing through mountains of "green" books pushing everything from "new world views" to "comprehensive agendas for planetary change", it's a breath of fresh air to come across an environmental book of the old school. That's not to say that Margaret Atherden's *Upland Britain* is out of touch, just that it takes you back to basics.

"The uplands are the last great refuge of wild nature in Britain," runs the foreword. The book tells the story of these areas. Be warned, this is no scenic stroll. For some, reading Atherden's book will be as hard as climbing the mountains she describes: The language is quite specialised and the tables will only be dwelt upon by students. But if you're one of those people fascinated by the processes which have created the countryside, then it's for you.

B

Rightly dubbed "the first classic of the modern environment movement," *Silent Spring* remains a book of extraordinary depth and prescience. If the campaign against DDT has been largely won in the developed world, there's still a fight going on in the South. But this is not just a book about the dangers of pesticides: it is an intensely evocative and powerful account of the rupture between ourselves and nature, and of the illusions peddled by politicians to justify that rupture.

C

I don't know off-hand how many adjectives and adverbs could legitimately be used to describe falling water, but I suspect Mary Welsh has all but emptied the store while guiding us to these 30 assorted spouts, gills, forces and falls.

Her aim is two-fold. She wants us to share her fascination with spumescent cataracts (that's a new one) and also her delight in birds and plants. Consequently the text reads more like a nature notebook than a walks guide.

That criticism aside, Mary Welsh writes a good deal better than most guidebook authors, while the complementary pen drawings by Linda Waters add their own charm. Most of the chosen waterfalls lie within gentle strolling distance of the road and, this being Yorkshire, you can expect a cathartic jolt from the contrast between the quaint and the bleak, the pastoral and the wild.

D

No animal inspires fear in humans quite like the great white shark. Whoever produces an effective shark repellent will become an overnight millionaire – and people are presently engaged in such a quest.

Yet, as Cousteau explains in this handsome book, the great white shark attacks human flesh only occasionally, probably for no better reason than that the flesh was in the way or that the shark wondered what it was.

In fact Cousteau found it difficult to attract sharks for his research, for not only are great whites threatened by commercial and sports fishing (increasingly popular since *Jaws*), but they also reproduce rarely.

Based at Dangerous Reef in southern Australia, a team of 40 experts studied the life of the great white for two-and-a-half years, tagging, tracking and observing from specially-built steel cages. This absorbing account of Cousteau's quest to understand this mysterious creature is terrifyingly illustrated.

E

In 1956 Chairman Mao took a swim in the Yangtze, the great river that effectively divides China in a line from Tibet to Shanghai. He was intent on reviving a project that had been smouldering since the 1920s: to harness the notoriously violent waters with a vast dam at the easterly end of the river's upper reaches, the breathtaking Three Gorges.

Decades on, the foundations of the Three Gorges dam are already being laid. If the project continues, it will be the biggest, most expensive dam in the world. Should it be a failure, as many experts predict, it would rank as one of the worst man-made disasters.

This and other similar tales of river exploitation – the proposed Mekong staircase of dams in Vietnam, superdams for Nepal for example – are the meat of Pearce's study. As the world's waterways seem set to become one of the great battlefields of the environmental movement in the Nineties, he points to the folly of numerous grandiose schemes. If we intend to replumb the planet, are we sure we know what we're doing?

F

The Gaia controversy rumbles on 14 years after this book first appeared. Lovelock has of course added much to his initial hypothesis (that the Earth is a living, self-regulating organism), but the elegance and freshness of the original text is a source of delight, and anything that rattles the scientific establishment like this must be a good thing.

G

The whale has come to symbolise everything that's both good and bad about our relationship with other creatures, and this wonderful book evokes the whale's life and being with unforgettable drama. But you can't just think all this green stuff; you've got to feel it, be seized by it, let go for it. Heathcote Williams's poetry does all of that with knobs on.

H

Farmer, poet, essayist, philosopher, naturalist, Wendell Berry is a real one-off. A love of the land combines with a love of the English language to produce that rarest combination of true profundity accessible to all. If every world leader had to spend a month working on Wendell Berry's farm in Kentucky, then we could do without any further Earth Summits! Reading him is the next best thing.

I

The message in Wilson's book is mostly not new: man is in imminent danger of precipitating a biological disaster of catastrophic proportions, as species disappear at the rate of 27,000 per year, 74 a day, three an hour.

Shock-horror statistics that we've all heard before. Yet probably never has the story of evolution been told as eloquently, or with such a galaxy of biological detail. We learn, for example, how spiders travel through the air, spinning web filaments long enough to be carried on the wind, like a balloon: and how the ultimate head-banger, the Californian acorn woodpecker, is adapted to save its brain from destruction; above all we learn of the importance of interdependency of species. Yet far from being depressing, this account of the world's complex evolution and current crisis is thoroughly inspiring. What can we do about it? Make an urgent survey of global biodiversity, says Wilson, before it's too late.

J

This book was first published in 1982 – but its re-release in paperback is welcome because it is still one of the most attractive and useful guides for amateur naturalists, especially those starting from scratch.

Part of the book is devoted to experiments in the home, such as how to dissect a cockroach, keep a snake or mount a skeleton. And for those who just want to read about some of the world's richest habitats, this book is an equally good companion.

10 40
10
10⁵⁵·

Read the following magazine article and answer questions **15–19**.

Science Writers

PITY the poor science writer. Richard Feynman, the most brilliant and influential physicist of our time, once said: "If you want to ... appreciate nature, it is necessary to understand the language she speaks in." That language is, of course, mathematics, which, Feynman noted, is "hard for some people".

Tough luck. "All the intellectual arguments that you can make will not communicate to deaf ears what the experience of music really is," he went on. "In the same way, all the intellectual arguments in the world will not convey an understanding of nature to those of 'the other culture'."

Let's call this Myth No 1: that science is a place apart; alien, the preserve of specialists, incomprehensible to the lay culture. If you don't have a ticket, you can't get in.

Myth No 2 is more subtle. It is that the principal task of the science writer is to popularise, to translate knowledge from one language (mathematics) to another (in this case, English), however imperfectly.

Myth No 3 is a cousin of the others: that the science writer must fall back on metaphor and poetry, like puffs of gauze, whereas the scientist builds with numbers and equations, like steel rods.

Like all good myths, they rest on half-truths. Mathematics *is* the language that nature speaks in, and much of science *has* grown distant from our common-sense understanding. Certainly, a science writer is haunted by the spectre of compromise, the feeling of having to filter a lush panorama through a flawed lens.

Yet how absurd it is to speak of science as something apart from our culture, from the fabric of ideas, traditions, languages and devices that surround us. If anything, in this century of the atomic bomb and the computer, of relativity and uncertainty and chaos, we are more deeply and knowledgeably embedded in a scientific world than ever before.

Perhaps because I came to science writing by accident, I have never believed that it is right to set out merely to *translate* science. It seems more useful to behave as any other writer does: to report news, if one is a news reporter, and to write history if one is a historian. Let the explanation follow behind.

When I wrote *Chaos*, an account of the recent evolution in scientists' understanding of complex systems, my intention – at least my primary intention – was not to explain the ideas, as one might hold a finished *objet d'art* up to the light. It was to tell the dramatic story of how a few people, at first mavericks in their fields, managed to transform the way scientists and the rest of us think about the world.

Science as we learn it in school is cut and dried. Not so in real life. Scientists make false steps, miscommunicate with colleagues, endure confusion. My goal was to let this science emerge for the reader as it had for these pioneers: gradually, in uncertain steps.

In *Genius*, I tried to write Feynman's biography as one would write the life of a politician, a painter, a cleric, or any other specialist in a discipline with its own jargon and tribal customs.

I believe that we have come to expect less from scientists' biographies than from those of others. We have tended to settle either for gross popularisations (Feynman's own anecdotal memoirs omitted the science that in reality he breathed from morning to night), or for stitched-together collections of technical explication; not biography at all.

Feynman's life in science encompassed far more than his profound contributions to quantum electrodynamics and other specific problems. I found myself drawn into the rapidly changing place of technology in our century's public life; the philosophy of scientific explanation, in a time so dominated by uncertainty; the role of visualisation in new scientific ideas; and the nature of genius itself.

And was it possible, in the end, to explain such subjects as quantum electrodynamics? Or does a science writer inevitably have to fall back on vague poetry? I'm not sure.

Feynman himself changed his mind during his lifetime, I discovered. He knew that the equations themselves are a kind of metaphor, always approximate, never final, a model for a more complex reality. They have a power for the scientist that mere words cannot have. But Feynman finally decided that it was possible to convey the essence of his physics even to those who could not do physics, to communicate music to deaf ears after all.

"To understand *how* subtraction works – as long as you don't actually have to carry it out – is not really so difficult," he said by way of analogy, a few years before his death.

"That's my position: I'm going to explain to you what the physicists are doing when they are predicting how nature will behave, but I'm not going to teach you any tricks so you can do it *efficiently*."

James Gleick, a former editor and science writer for the 'New York Times', is the author of 'Genius: Richard Feynman and Modern Physics'.

15 Gleick's purpose in quoting Feynman at the beginning of the article is to

    A demonstrate his own intellectual qualities.
    B illustrate 'Myth No. 1'.
    C show that Feynman was an exceptional scientist.
    D explain how the 'Myths' were created.

16 Gleick suggests these 'Myths' are only half true because

    A science writing is a common-sense compromise.
    B we know that science is not separate from our everyday lives.
    C the pace of change has accelerated enormously.
    D scientific discoveries have changed the way we live.

17 What does Gleick perceive his job to be?

    A to give an account of scientific developments
    B to describe scientific theories
    C to change people's perception of science
    D to prevent the public from being deceived by scientists

18 What was Gleick's aim when writing Feynman's biography?

    A to describe both the man and his work
    B to show that scientists are just like other professional people
    C to explain Feynman's work
    D to account for Feynman's exceptional success

19 What did Feynman change his mind about?

    A how to explain quantum electrodynamics
    B whether non-scientists can understand science
    C the importance of literature
    D the best way to describe complex ideas

Remember to put your answers on the separate answer sheet.

THIRD TEXT / QUESTIONS 20–25

*Read this magazine article, then choose the best paragraph from **A–G** to fill each of the gaps **20–25**. There is one extra paragraph which does not belong in any of the gaps.*

A round 30 years ago canoeists decided to move indoors to the comfort and convenience of the swimming pool for training. Initially these pool sessions were used to introduce beginners to the sport and to give more experienced canoeists the chance to perfect more advanced techniques.

20

Paddlers compete in a head to head race, with two identical courses being set up down the length of a pool. The course is defined by pairs of poles hung one metre apart which must be negotiated in a specific order and direction.

21

Others looking to add to their general training took a different route and at many pools they introduced a ball to provide extra interest. Before too long you had the beginnings of the game that was to become canoe polo.

22

Goals are scored in a 1 x 1.5m. net goal suspended 2m. above the ends. A water polo ball is used and the canoes are just 3m. long for use in confined space.

23

The game itself resembles basketball on water, except for the start – the teams line up at opposite ends of the pool facing each other, a referee throws the ball into the centre of the pool and one member of each team sprints for it.

24

A player with the ball can expect to be tackled in a variety of ways – either by being pushed by hand or by an opponent trying to unbalance them.

Games are relatively short, with two halves of between 6 and 10 minutes each way.

25

The regional leagues feed into a series of national leagues, which are organised in four divisions. As with Pool Slalom there is a National Championship, run on a knock-out basis. The atmosphere, from the local eliminating rounds to the finals, is always excellent.

A

Canoe polo in the UK now has approximately 1,000 participants playing in regionally based leagues. Players at the start of a career in canoe polo typically have only the most rudimentary canoeing ability, with most clubs more than happy to teach both general canoeing as well as polo skills.

B

Division 1 contains ten teams from as far afield as Southampton and Glasgow, the other leagues split into north and south. There are dedicated leagues for women and under 18's.

C

Gradually, pool canoeing became an end in itself. As part of the process of teaching, poles or gates would be erected. Soon races through a series of gates were held and the sport of pool slalom was born.

D

By the early seventies there was a British National Championship and versions of the game were being played across Europe and in Australia. A major step forward was taken in 1985 with the creation of internationally accepted rules:

E

From there on the ball is passed by hand, though paddles are used for ball control, the interception of passes and for blocking shots.

F

There are time penalties for touching a pole or missing a gate. Canoeists of all abilities are encouraged to enter the National Championships.

G

Teams consist of up to eight players, but only five are allowed in the playing area at any one time. Substitution can be made at any time, even during play.

Remember to put your answers on the separate answer sheet.

1⁹⁵·

FOURTH TEXT / QUESTIONS 26–33

Answer questions **26–33** *by referring to the magazine article on page 72.*

For questions **26–30**, *choose the* **positive** *aspects of the micropropagation of plants mentioned in the article, from list* **A–H** *below.*

Positive aspects mentioned:

	A	produces more abundant crops
26	**B**	means that the public has rapid access to new plant varieties
27	**C**	produces young plants which do not have diseases
	D	speeds up research
28	**E**	offers higher profit margins for plant breeders
29	**F**	can aid the conservation of endangered plant species
30	**G**	results in easier working conditions for foresters
	H	can produce plants which resist attack by certain pests

For questions **31–33**, *choose the* **negative** *aspects of the micropropagation of plants mentioned in the article, from list* **A–F** *below.*

Negative aspects mentioned:

	A	is not a practical possibility for some plants
31	**B**	could lead to practices which reduce the variety of plants and animals
	C	creates crops which are vulnerable to wholesale destruction by pests
32	**D**	is causing the market to become flooded with new species
33	**E**	may lead to a reduction in the workforce
	F	may lead to the creation of forests which support no other living things

---

Remember to put your answers on the separate answer sheet.

Micropropagation

If you've bought a garden plant recently, the odds are that it started life as a green blob in a sterile dish in a laboratory. Micropropagation – the rapid multiplication of plants using tissue-culture technology – is becoming big business.

One of its advantages is speed. Take a small piece of plant, put it in a medium which encourages it to form multiple shoots, then repeat the exercise.

One plant becomes tens of thousands or even millions in a matter of months. And every copy of the plant is a genetically uniform clone.

This can be a boon to horticulturists and gardeners. New varieties reach the market place in record time, and the technique also generates disease-free stock. Micropropagation is also playing an increasingly important role in the conservation of rare plants. But there is one application that carries a serious ecological risk.

Micropropagation of forest trees is a superficially attractive proposition. Most tree species show enormous variability in growth rates, shape and almost every other economically important character. Conventional selective-breeding methods to improve them are at best slow and at worst completely impractical. Breeders may have to wait 10 years before they can assess the performance of new varieties. Some species, such as oaks, may take 40 years to produce the crop of seeds that will show whether desirable characters will be inherited.

But micropropagation could soon change all that. By cloning in a test tube the biggest and best trees, plantations could be established with a limited range of varieties that satisfy commercial forestry's narrow criteria for the ideal tree. Tissue culture technologists have already begun to clone

eucalyptus, oak, birch, poplar, willow, pine and fir.

These developments also pave the way for new possibilities for genetic engineering in forestry. Experimental poplars which contain foreign genes that give insect and herbicide resistance already exist.

If all this goes strictly according to plan, we could look forward to a new breed of weed-free, insect-free forests of cloned trees – a sterile habitat formed from shoots multiplied in sterile culture.

That's the medium-term risk. The longer-term hazard arises if it all goes wrong and the pests and diseases retaliate. The history of international agriculture is littered with examples of famine and disasters precipitated by epidemics of insects, fungi and bacteria that have mutated and overwhelmed the man-manipulated defences of genetically uniform crops. As I write, the grape vines in California's Napa Valley, which are clonally propagated by cuttings, are being sucked dry by a new strain of aphid.

This is why maintaining diversity in crops is at least as important as conserving biodiversity in natural ecosystems. It's our only long-term insurance policy against such disasters.

Sudden pest 'pandemics' affecting monocultures of tree clones would be particularly damaging. Slow-growing forests occupy land that remains relatively undisturbed for decades. This accumulates a wider range of plant and animal species and has a much higher ecological value than land disturbed by annual cycles of intensive cropping.

While the sudden loss of an annual crop usually has little effect on wildlife, the consequences of a rapid decline of a species can be dramatic. It may be that someone, somewhere, is assessing the potential risks that micropropagation in forestry holds for wildlife, and that these will be balanced against commercial advantage. But somehow, I doubt it.

PAPER 2 WRITING (2 hours)

This paper contains one Section A task and four Section B tasks. You must complete the Section A task and one task from Section B.

SECTION A

1 A few weeks ago you enrolled for the language course marked on the price list below. Yesterday you received a letter from the language school as shown. You discussed this problem with an English colleague. On arriving at work this morning, you found a note from him on your desk. **Using the information given**, write the letters and note listed below.

LIGHTFOOT LANGUAGE SERVICES
Advanced course dates and prices

W/3/A	January 15 – April 3	£1750	✔
SP/3/A	April 17 – June 30	£1800	
S/1/A	July 1 – July 28	£700	
S/X/A	July 30 – August 15	£500	
A/3/A	September 10 – December 10	£1800	

Note: A deposit of £150 is payable on booking. The remainder of the fee is payable not less than two weeks before the beginning of the course. The deposit is not normally refundable.

LIGHTFOOT LANGUAGE SERVICES
RENTON ROAD WARMSLEY LONDON SW21 5JJ
Tel. 081-752-9790

11th November

Dear Sir or Madam,
With reference to your booking for our advanced course 15th January — 3rd April next year, we regret to inform you that this course will not be available. We offer our sincere apologies for any inconvenience this may cause you. We have registered your name for our next course (SP/3/A) instead, at no extra charge, and trust that this will be convenient for you.

Yours faithfully,

M. Pullen
Matthew Pullen
Principal

Thurs am

I've been thinking over what you told me yesterday about the language school letting you down over dates. I think it'd be worth your writing to the place where I used to teach. They have an advanced course roughly when you want to go. They're very fussy about the standard of people they take – you have to be pretty serious! – and they are a bit more expensive, BUT I think if you write to Mrs Norman, saying I suggested it, & explain what happened with the other place, they might be prepared to give you a bit of a discount. Tell them a bit about yourself as well – they always ask prospective students to do that. It'd certainly be worth a try. It's a very good school, too. The address is Executive Language Centre, Wooley Hall, Wooley, London NW10 3XW.

Good luck!
   George Abbott

ps. Don't forget to make sure you get your deposit back – it's their fault, after all.

Now write

(a) a **letter** to Lightfoot Language Services, cancelling your booking (about 50 words)

(b) a **letter** to Mrs Norman, as advised by your colleague (about 150 words)

(c) a **note** to your colleague, thanking him for his advice and saying what you have done (about 50 words)

You must set them out in an appropriate way but it is not necessary to include addresses.

SECTION B

*Choose **ONE** of the following writing tasks. Your answer should follow exactly the instructions given. You are advised to write approximately 250 words.*

2 Your language school/workplace was recently visited by a famous person. You have been asked by an English language newspaper to write **an account of the visit**. Explain who the visitor was, the purpose of the visit, what happened and how you and your friends felt about the event.

3 You have just finished reading a book which was recommended to you by a friend. Write **a letter** thanking her/him for telling you about it. Give your opinion of it, and suggest a book which you think your friend might like, explaining your reasons for recommending it.

4 The company you work for recruits employees from several different countries. Your boss has asked you to **contribute to a leaflet** which she is putting together for new arrivals. Your section will be entitled 'Dos & Don'ts'. You can cover matters such as punctuality, sick leave, confidentiality, dress, or anything else which might be useful to employees unfamiliar with your culture.

5 You decide to go in for this competition which you see in a magazine. Write **your entry**.

WIN A FORTNIGHT'S **FREE** TUITION AT A TOP FILM SCHOOL!

PLUS
A STATE-OF-THE-ART VIDEO CAMERA WITH ALL THE EXTRAS

Simply send us a description of the half-hour film you would like to make about your town or village. In 250 words, tell us what you would like to show and why.

Send your entry to: **Euro Video, 35 Panton Street, Birmingham, England** to reach us by the end of the month.

PAPER 3 ENGLISH IN USE (1 hour 30 minutes)

Answer all questions.

SECTION A

1 *For questions **1–15**, read the text below and decide which word below and on page 62 best fits each space. Put the letter you choose for each question in the correct box on your answer sheet. The exercise begins with an example (**0**).*

WHALING

Rock carvings suggest that Stone Age people were hunting whales for food as (**0**) ... as 2200 BC. Such (**1**) ... hunting is still practised today in a number of (**2**) ... including the Inuit people of Greenland and North America.

Whaling became big (**3**) ... from the seventeenth century as the (**4**) ... for whalebone and whale oil rose, and humpback and sperm whales were hunted in (**5**) ... large numbers. But just as (**6**) ... of these species began to fall, the explosive harpoon-gun was (**7**) ... . This weapon, together with the development of steam-powered ships, (**8**) ... the whalers to hunt the fast-moving fin and blue whales.

In 1905 the whaling (**9**) ... moved to the waters of Antarctica. The introduction of (**10**) ... factory ships enabled the whales to be processed at sea. As a result the blue whale had (**11**) ... disappeared by the 1950s. In 1946 the International Whaling Commission was (**12**) ... to maintain the declining whale populations. Quotas were (**13**) ... but these were often (**14**) ... and numbers continued to fall. Hunting of many species continued until 1986 when the IWC finally responded to international (**15**) ... and a ban on commercial whaling was introduced.

0	**A** soon	**B** long	**C** early	**D** distant
1	**A** survival	**B** essential	**C** basic	**D** subsistence
2	**A** groups	**B** societies	**C** races	**D** nationalities
3	**A** business	**B** commerce	**C** trade	**D** finance
4	**A** demand	**B** desire	**C** request	**D** reliance
5	**A** repeatedly	**B** frequently	**C** continually	**D** increasingly
6	**A** stores	**B** stocks	**C** supplies	**D** assets
7	**A** invented	**B** discovered	**C** assembled	**D** applied
8	**A** managed	**B** employed	**C** enabled	**D** empowered

Visual Material for Paper 5

1A

1B

1C

1D

1F

1E

1G

1H

1J

1K

1L

1M

1P

2A

2C

3A

2B

4A

2D

2E

A driving range – in your back garden

This ingenious golf trainer lets you work on your game with no more broken windows or lost balls! It consists of a ball suspended from a steel arm by a virtually unbreakable nylon cord. When you hit the ball it precisely indicates the direction of the shot, helping you to correct your swing. Every golfer should have one!

• **Golf Swing Trainer £37.50 KA15471**

Peel fruit without the effort

Peeling fruit can be a tiring, time-consuming task. But at last there's now a way to finish it off with a minimum of effort. You can use the Electric Peeler in much the same way as a traditional one – except that as you pass the blade over the vegetable it peels automatically. Powered by 2 × AA batteries (not supplied). Measures 9¼″ long.

• **Electric Peeler £10.95 TK973**

Instant solution for too-tight clothes

When clothes get too tight for comfort, reach for Wonder Buttons! The discreet Wonder Button instantly adds around half a size. For skirts, the 19mm buttons can be used, while the 15mm trouser version gives button-top jeans or trousers a more forgiving fit! All three are made from aluminium and stainless steel with a nylon stretch-stop inside the spring.

• **Wonder Buttons (3) £5.99 KA16548**

• **Wonder Buttons (6) £9.99 KA17629**

Give yourself a facelift!

To stay in shape, face and neck muscles need just as much exercise as those elsewhere in your body, but they're difficult to train and often neglected. Now you can use the superb Sleek Cheeks exerciser to help fight wrinkles and double chins. The handsets work by transmitting tiny electrical pulses into the muscles, stimulating muscles in a safe and gentle way. Full instructions and batteries supplied.

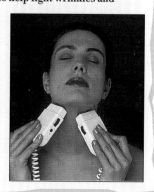

• **Sleek Cheeks £42.95 TP733A**

C7

3B

4C

3C

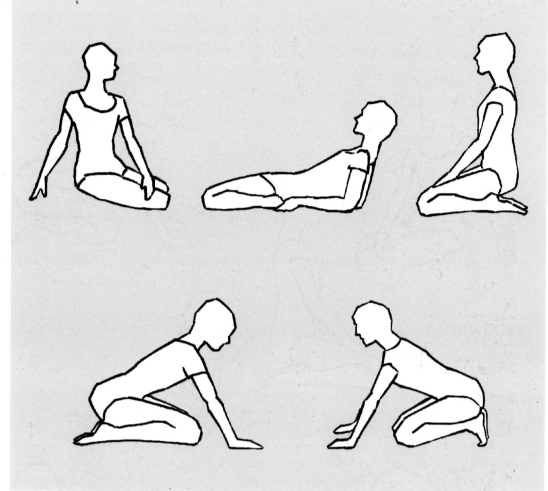

4E

NO MORE POLLUTION

NO MORE PAIN

NO MORE UNEMPLOYMENT

NO MORE ILLITERACY

ANTARCTICA: CAPE TO CAPE

Cape Town to Cape Horn - a 24 day voyage of adventure

Departing 6 December

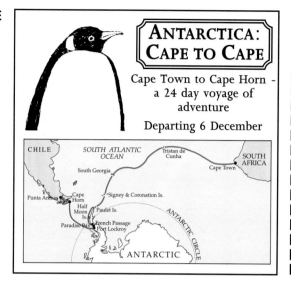

DISCOVER THE MEDITERRANEAN IN THE SPRINGTIME

Our cruises are carefully planned to balance time for relaxation on board, with guided tours and time for independent sightseeing ashore.

SAMARKAND *to* BUKHARA

A visit to the great bazaars, oases, hidden treasures and sights of the Silk Road with a special direct flight service from London to Tashkent

CHINA COASTAL CRUISE

THE YANGTSE AND BEYOND

A visit to Hong Kong – Xiamen – Fuzhou – Shanghai – Zhangjiang – Nanjing – Hangzhou – Xian –

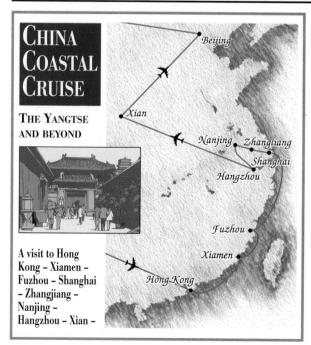

ISLAND AND PENINSULA

FROM SINGAPORE TO PENANG
12 days from £795
Visiting: Singapore – Malacca – Kuala Lumpur – Cameron Highlands – Penang

4B

4D

9	A lines	B troops	C staff	D fleets
10	A sturdy	B bulky	C massive	D gross
11	A virtually	B possibly	C uniquely	D commonly
12	A assumed	B expected	C inspired	D established
13	A made	B set	C placed	D done
14	A refused	B denied	C ignored	D exempted
15	A reputation	B volume	C shame	D pressure

Do not forget to put your answers on the answer sheet.

Example:

0	C		0
			▭ ▭

2 *For questions* **16–30**, *complete the following text by writing each missing word on your answer sheet.* **Use only one word for each space.** *The exercise begins with an example* **(0).**

ART AS A CAREER

Many celebrated artists have found it hard to make ends meet early **(0)** ... in their careers. **(16)** ... a few well-known exceptions, however, (poor van Gogh being perhaps the most famous one) **(17)** ... went on to find recognition within their **(18)** ... lifetime. Picasso's life story is the kind of rags-to-riches tale **(19)** ... gives hope to many **(20)** ... unknown artist. In 1904, he was sharing a draughty and primitive studio complex **(21)** ... thirty other artists. But by his death, he was a multi-millionaire and probably the most celebrated modern artist **(22)** ... . Nevertheless, **(23)** ... every success story, there must be dozens of artists (perhaps some potential 'greats') **(24)** ... have endured a lifetime **(25)** ... hardship in obscurity. **(26)** ... they were never recognised because their work was **(27)** ... of sympathy with the prevailing fashion, or because they lacked talent, **(28)** ... is impossible to say. Most people see art as a vocation rather than a career. There **(29)** ... indeed be some truth in the idea that artists need to be exceptionally dedicated to succeed, and even relatively successful artists sometimes have to supplement their income **(30)** ... working in other areas occasionally.

Do not forget to put your answers on the answer sheet.

Example:

0	on		0
			▭ ▭

SECTION B

3 *In **most** lines of the following text, there is either **one** spelling or **one***
*punctuation error. For each numbered line **31–43**, write the correctly spelled*
word or show the correct punctuation on your answer sheet. Some lines are
correct. Indicate these lines with a tick (✓). The exercise begins with three
examples (0).

AN ASTRONOMY LECTURE

0	A well-known scientist once gave a public lecture on astronomy. He described
0	how the earth orbits around the sun and how the sun, in turn orbits around the
0	centre of a vast collection of stars called our gallaxy. At the end of the lecture,
31	a little old lady at the back of the room got up and said: 'What you have told
32	us is rubbish? The world is really a flat plate supported on the back of a
33	giant tortoise.' The scientist gave a superior smile before replying, 'What is
34	the tortoise standing on?' 'You're very clever, young man, very clever, said
35	the old lady. 'But its tortoises all the way down!'
36	Most people would find the picture of our universe as an infinite tower of
37	tortoises rather ridiculous, but why do we think, we know better? What
38	do we know about the universe and how do we know it? Recent
39	breakthroughs in physiques, made possible in part by fantastic new
40	technologies; suggest answers to some of our oldest questions. One
41	day these answers may seem as obvious to us as the earth orbiting the
42	sun – or perhaps as ridiculous as a tower of tortoises: only time (whatever
43	that maybe) will tell.

Do not forget to put your answers on the answer sheet.

Example:

0	✓	0 ▭ ▭
0	**in turn, orbits**	0 ▭ ▭
0	**galaxy**	0 ▭ ▭

4 For questions **44–54**, read the following extract from an informal letter
about problems with a magazine subscription and use the information to
complete the numbered gaps in the formal letter of complaint. Then write
the new words in the correct spaces on your answer sheet. **Use no more
than two words** for each gap. The exercise begins with an example **(0)**. The
words you need **do not occur** in the informal letter.

INFORMAL LETTER

Dear Isobel,

*Sorry it's taken so long to answer your last letter, but I've been a bit busy.
Apart from college etc, you won't believe the hassles I've been having trying
to cancel that magazine New Worlds! It all started when Mum gave me a
subscription as a birthday present a couple of years ago. It was OK at
first, I was fairly into astronomy and stuff at the time, well, still am, of
course, but by the end of a year I realised I knew all the sorts of stuff they
have. So I decided to get something a bit more serious, a proper scientific
journal. I thought if I just didn't pay the sub, they'd stop sending the mag.
But it wasn't that simple. They kept on sending it, and then I got these
notes telling me I hadn't paid, which I just chucked in the bin. Then I got
this letter offering me two years' cheap subscription. Then I got a rather
nasty note – it was about six months on, threatening all sorts of trouble
from their lawyers if I didn't pay for the mags I'd had. So I wrote and told
them I didn't ask for their stupid magazines etc. Now I've had another rude
letter, so I've written to the boss and told him that if they don't leave me in
peace, it'll be me who's calling in the lawyers, not them! I hope it works.
Anyway, how are things with you ...*

FORMAL LETTER

Dear Mr Wallis,

I am writing to clarify the situation **(0)** ... my subscription to your magazine 'New Worlds', as your mailing department seems to **(44)** ... some confusion about it.

 Two years ago, I **(45)** ... a year's subscription. I enjoyed the magazine, but as I am now studying physics at university, I felt that it was no **(46)** ... appropriate to me. Consequently, I did **(47)** ... the subscription last year. Unfortunately, your mailing department **(48)** ... to dispatch copies of the magazine, and to **(49)** ... . Naturally, I **(50)** ... these demands, as I had not ordered the magazine.

 Two months ago, I received a letter offering me two years' subscription at **(51)** ..., and shortly afterwards another which appeared to threaten **(52)** ... action for failing to pay my account.

 I am extremely annoyed at **(53)** ... in this outrageous manner and if I do not receive your immediate **(54)** ... that the matter is closed, I shall contact my solicitor.

Yours sincerely,

Teresa Marks

Do not forget to put your answers on the answer sheet.

Example:

0	regarding	0
		▢ ▢

SECTION C

5 *For questions **55–63**, read through the following text and then choose from list **A–M** the best phrase or sentence given below it to fill each of the blanks. Write one letter **(A–M)** in the correct box on your answer sheet. **Some of the suggested answers do not fit at all**. One answer has been given as an example **(0)**.*

WELLS AND BENNETT

During their lifetimes, H G Wells and Arnold Bennett achieved a public fame of a kind that has been accorded to **(0)** ... before or since. They would not have had it if **(55)** ..., and yet the nature of the fame **(56)** ... as such. It was essentially that of the journalist, the popular pundit **(57)** ... with complete self-assurance. With Shaw, **(58)** ... was also a product of journalism, they divided between them the empire of the press, **(59)** ... .

All that **(60)** ... as novelists. Both were men **(61)** ... in fiction, to say nothing of their short stories, Wells wrote nearly fifty novels, Bennett thirty. Of these, perhaps ten of Wells's are still valuable **(62)** ..., if the best of the scientific romances are included, and, **(63)** ..., five of Bennett's.

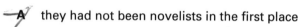

A   they had not been novelists in the first place

B   prepared to pronounce on any subject under the sun

C   the most highly paid writers in the Anglo-Saxon world

D   has nothing to do with their merit

E   more certainly

F   in their own right,

G   of vast output

H   if they had wanted to

I   is generally acknowledged

J   whose popular reputation

K   had little to do with their novels

L   was undeniably

M   no other English novelist

Do not forget to put your answers on the answer sheet.

Example:

0	M		0

6 *Use the following notes to write out details of travel and accommodation arrangements for delegates who will be attending a conference which you are helping to organise in London. Write **one complete sentence** on the answer sheet for each numbered set of notes, using connecting words and phrases as appropriate. You may add words and change the form of the words given in the notes but do not add any extra information. The first point has been expanded for you as an example **(0)**.*

London Language Conference

0 Below:- details your travel/accommodation arrangements

81 Responsibility sponsors organise/pay travel to London.

82 Stay Atlantic Hotel 5 mins underground (Lancaster Gate stn).

83 Cost underground refundable (**_not_** taxi)

84 Check in hotel 7–9pm, identify self as delegate Lang. Conf. (collect meal vouchers)

85 Main conf. centre = Merton Hall, (corner Merton Place)

86 If not familiar London – directions hotel porter

87 Arrive Hall 8.30 – time for admin – 1st session start prompt 9 am

---

The space below can be used for your rough answers.
Do not forget to put your answers on the answer sheet.

Dear Colleague,

London Language Conference

0 Please see below for details of your travel and accommodation arrangements.

81

82

83

84

85

86

87

PAPER 4 LISTENING (45 minutes)

Answer all questions.

*Jim has called his business partner, Ed, to tell him about some ideas for altering their office. For questions **1–8** listen to what Jim says and complete Ed's notes.*

You will hear the recording twice.

Office alterations?

Knock down wall of _____ **1**

Hide work area with screen at _____ **2** height

Large work surface as desk and for _____ **3**

Cupboards along wall in _____ **4**

Space in work area for phone and _____ **5**

Lights: in _____ **6** above table

in _____ **7** above work surface

Ventilation: fan in _____ **8**

SECTION B

You will hear a local radio announcement about travel conditions. For questions **9–17** *look at the pictures and mark* **YES** *the problems which are described. Mark the ones which are* **NOT** *described* **NO**.

Listen very carefully as you will hear this piece only ONCE.

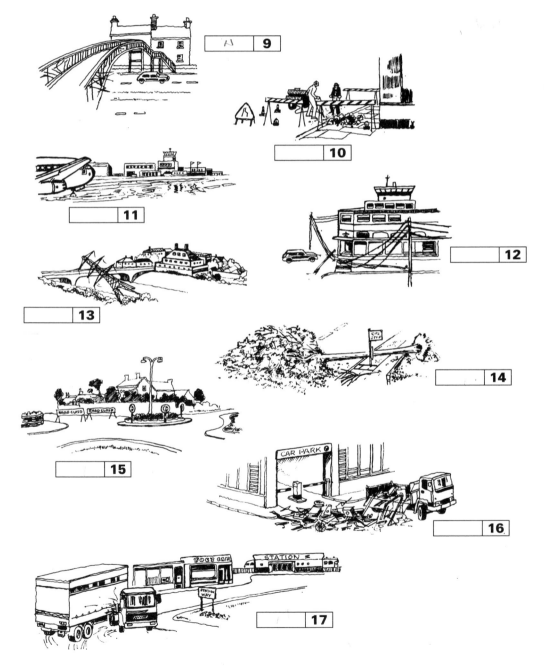

SECTION C

You will hear part of a radio programme in which James Clebourne, the award-winning photographer, talks to the presenter, Miranda Day, about his early life and the beginnings of his successful career. For questions 18–26, complete the information according to what James says.

You will hear the piece twice.

When his parents died, James felt [_____ **18**]

James felt the punishments he received from his uncle and aunt were
[_____ **19**]

The quality he inherited from his father was [_____ **20**]

The quality he inherited from his mother was [_____ **21**]

His choice of career made his uncle feel [_____ **22**]

At first this made James feel [_____ **23**]

Later he began to feel [_____ **24**]

His choice of career made his aunt feel [_____ **25**]

His present relationship with his aunt resulted from the actions of
[_____ **26**]

SECTION D

You will hear extracts of five different people talking about a near disaster at an airport. A plane which was approaching the area had to make an emergency landing in poor weather conditions. The people are describing how the event affected them.

Task one

Letters A–H list various different people. As you listen, put them in order by completing the boxes numbered 27–31 with the appropriate letter.

Task two

Letters A–H list the main ideas expressed by the speakers. As you listen, put them in order by completing the boxes numbered 32–36 with the appropriate letter.

You will hear the series twice.

Task one

A   the pilot

B   a passenger

C   a steward

D   an airport fire officer

E   a check-in clerk

F   the manager of the airport restaurant

G   a taxi driver

H   a customs officer

	27
	28
	29
	30
	31

Task two

A   We didn't realise anything was wrong.

B   I didn't have time to feel scared.

C   I followed the usual procedure in such conditions.

D   I'm glad I didn't have to get involved.

E   It was unfair that I had to do all the explaining.

F   We weren't really prepared for such a situation.

G   I had to work a lot of extra hours.

H   We couldn't do our job properly.

	32
	33
	34
	35
	36

Note: For Paper 5 see pages 148–149 and the Colour Section.

Practice Test 4

PAPER 1 READING (1 hour 15 minutes)

Answer all questions.

FIRST TEXT / QUESTIONS 1–13

*Answer questions **1–13** below by referring to the profiles of young engineers on pages 88–89.*

*For questions **1–8** match each person with the appropriate facts **A–H**.*
*Note: Where there is more than one fact about a person they can be given **in any order**.*

Hannah	1	2	3 ....
Mark	4	5	
Christine	6	7	8 ....

This young engineer

- **A** gets involved in negotiations with suppliers of equipment.
- **B** uses computers to plan new developments.
- **C** sometimes has to work quickly under pressure.
- **D** keeps a check on how equipment is functioning over a period of time.
- **E** tries to solve problems which affect people's everyday lives.
- **F** re-designs existing equipment to meet new specifications.
- **G** is involved in work which reduces pollution.
- **H** helps people who use computers to check equipment.

*For questions **9–13** match each person with the appropriate statements **A–E**.*
*Note: Where there is more than one fact about a person, they can be given **in any order**.*

Hannah	9		
Mark	10	11	12 ....
Christine	13		

This young engineer

- **A** feels the work contributes to economic progress.
- **B** originally planned to be a doctor.
- **C** enjoys persuading other people to work hard.
- **D** chose to work in this field without really knowing what it involved.
- **E** thinks the job is more exciting than outsiders realise.

Remember to put your answers on the separate answer sheet.

Young engineers

A

Hannah Reynolds, 26, HNC in engineering from North Lincolnshire College, senior development engineer, British Airways

HANNAH REYNOLDS was aiming for medicine when something changed her mind. "In the final year of my physics A-level, there was a module on electronics. I enjoyed it so much that I decided to give up medicine and pursue engineering. I preferred it because it is so 'hands on'."

At British Airways, Hannah works on the computer systems that run an aircraft, such as the cockpit displays that tell pilots what is happening in their aircraft, and allow them to control and monitor everything from the fuel to passengers' oxygen supplies.

Hannah provides technical support to the avionics workshop; it is office and computer-based. When a piece of equipment is thought by the pilot to be faulty, it is taken off the aircraft and sent to the workshop for testing, usually by highly-automated, computerised test equipment. Hannah helps design improvements to the test equipment, and to monitor trends and reliability.

"If two or three components are all failing in the same way or at the same time, we have to go to the manufacturer to talk about alternatives or solutions."

Though she is studying for a master's degree in business, Hannah aims to get as broad a range of engineering experience as she can in the airline industry. Possibilities include operations, which involves work on aircraft due to fly within hours, and heavy maintenance, where aircraft come into the hangar to be stripped bare on a regular basis.

At her level, Hannah is not taking a spanner to planes, but organising, scheduling, coordinating and providing high level technical expertise: variety is one of the main attractions of Hannah's job.

"No two days are ever alike. And the engineering field is changing literally every day. There is no opportunity to get bored."

B

Mark Lansley, 30, degree in chemical engineering from Leeds University, project engineer with Glaxochem

MARK works in a factory making the active ingredients for antibiotics. His job is to design and build chemical plant, co-ordinating the input of a wide range of people – draughtsmen, chemical, electronics and instrument engineers, people concerned with health, safety and quality – to get the plant up and running.

Much work centres on equipment that is already there: "You may have to change things to meet new EC regulations or reduce costs, or to make improvements in conditions or capacity or speed."

He normally works on several projects at a time. At present they include work on reducing the factory's waste, recycling chemicals, automating a repetitive job, improving a filter system to increase capacity, and the computer control of chemical plant. Different things have excited him during his career. "At first I really got a buzz from technical things, seeing how things worked, really getting to the bottom of them. Then I got into designing equipment. Running up and down stairs to see valves open and close precisely when software I'd written said they should – it was a real thrill.

"A year in production changed my outlook. I was moving away from the equipment to managing people. That gave me a new buzz, to initiate an objective and then manage the people to achieve it. You need to motivate and communicate, to be enthusiastic. It's great to see someone who was not enthusiastic turn around, begin to come in early, work late, show you what they've done."

Mark enjoys the pleasure of being creative, solving problems, and of producing things. He is keenly aware of his wealth-creating role. He also travels widely – to Singapore, Germany, The Netherlands, Switzerland: "It's glamorous. That may not be the image people have, but it is."

c

Christine Thompson, 24, degree in civil engineering from Loughborough University, employed by Oscar Faber TPA

TRANSPORT engineering is not just the hidden face of engineering; it is very nearly the hidden face of civil engineering, of which it is a specialisation. The sandwich placement of her degree course put Christine Thompson off "straight" civil engineering, but when she opted instead for transport, she had no idea what she had let herself in for.

In explaining transport engineering, Christine likes to quote her boss: "If it moves, we're interested in it – pedestrians, cars, lorries, planes, ships." Though she considers herself a jack-of-all-trades, Christine's job has two main components: transportation modelling and traffic engineering.

Transportation engineering uses computer models to predict the amount of traffic that is going to use roads. Preliminary surveys involve interviewing people about their journeys – the start, the finish, the reason. Results are fed into the computer. By adding new roads to the model of existing roads and traffic, you can see what will happen in different situations.

Traffic engineering is the nitty-gritty of designing roads and junctions. Christine may be called in to help

sort out a junction that is not working. "After looking at cars using the junction, where they come from, where they exit, and using a computer model, a range of options is developed. They could include, for example, a new signalling sequence, or a roundabout."

Christine enjoys the mix. "Modelling can take several years because of the scale and intricacy. It really takes time fully to understand what's involved. Traffic is much more immediate, short-term and intense. You might have to design a junction in a week. It gives me a buzz, but you couldn't do it all the time, you'd get worn out." She is learning all the time, and her job offers enormous scope for specialisation. "I also feel I'm doing some good in the long run; that my work has a social value."

SECOND TEXT / QUESTIONS 14–19

Read the following magazine article and answer questions **14–19**.

Tasmin Little

Musical prodigies, as far as violin players are concerned, are by no means a recent phenomenon and today's bumper crop of juvenile fiddlers is enough to encourage even the most cynical commentator to delve deep into his stockpile of superlatives. However, the strong suspicion remains that most technically gifted teenagers fall short when it comes to conveying the emotional depths of the violin repertoire.

At 27, Tasmin Little may appear slightly long in the tooth beside the striplings presently appearing in the most distinguished musical company. The London-born violinist, however, is beginning to attract press and public acclaim, not for her lack of years or off-stage antics, but for the insight and maturity of her performances. Little's credentials as a player are impeccable, developed first at the Menuhin School before further training at the Guildhall School of Music and in Canada. Her professional career has survived record company and media hype and exposure.

Talk of ambition and career development elicits a level-headed response from Little, who seems very happy with the way things have progressed so far. 'Of course, there are certain pieces I'm itching to play and to record. I think the secret is not to want everything at once. You can't possibly play the whole repertoire in the first few years of a career; if you did, you'd have nowhere left to go. I temper my desires with a touch of realism. I know the things I'm capable of now, and those I should work at, to allow me to continue to improve.' Far from allowing the grass to grow under her, Little has already tackled a healthy slice of the concerto repertoire, working with numerous distinguished conductors both in the concert hall and on disc.

She is adamant that the success or failure of any performance lies in its preparation. Her own interpretations are usually shaped over suitably long periods and not committed to disc until she feels she has something to say and the means with which to say it. 'When I started out as a soloist, I was pretty green. I've since worked on technique and learned from my mistakes, but I've also lived a bit as well; I've had experiences, some sad, some happy. You can't hope to portray unhappiness in music unless you've had some taste of it yourself. The really great performers are able to move their audience and they are prepared to expose their souls.'

What of the future? Since her first Proms* appearance in 1990, Little has rapidly ascended several steps on the career ladder, but admits that the next step up is the most important and tricky of all to negotiate. Clearly, she is aware that her reputation abroad is less developed than at home, although she is concerned that in the process of moving into the major league of international artists she does not restrict the variety and range of repertoire. 'It seems that today you have to do things as quickly as possible, reach the top and stay there. Of course, I want to get there, to play with all the major orchestras and conductors, but I would be much happier to have a bit of fun along the way. I want to enjoy the voyage as much as the arrival.'

Making her latest disc, of the Brahms and Sibelius concertos, was a particularly rewarding if somewhat painful experience. 'My fingers began to bleed when we were recording the last movement of the Sibelius, but I didn't let that stop me. I couldn't possibly have done something like that disc at the beginning of my career. When it came to the test, I had a lot of experience on which to draw. I was shattered but very pleased by the end of the session. Although it's probably immodest to say so, I think the atmosphere in the first movement of the Sibelius

*Proms: a famous London concert series

is really something quite special.'

With seven discs now under her belt, she feels that the general improvement in her playing is, in part, a positive by-product of working in the studio. Listening to tape playbacks, Little says, allows her to be far more objective about matters of technique and expression than when she's actually performing. 'That's the only way to learn and to improve. Doing concerts, you never properly listen to yourself. Recordings give you the chance to find out exactly where you're going wrong. I find that's a tremendously liberating experience, one which allows me to confirm or alter my feelings about a piece.'

14 How is Tasmin Little said to differ from other young violinists?

    A Success has come to her earlier than to most.
    B Her technical ability is exceptionally good.
    C Her playing shows emotional maturity.
    D She has had a lot of attention from the media.

15 What is Little's attitude to her future career?

    A She is prepared to be patient.
    B She is frustrated that she can't do more recording.
    C She is ambitious to record with famous conductors.
    D She will concentrate on perfecting her performance skills.

16 What does Little feel should be the attitude of a great musician?

    A The audience has the right to expect a flawless performance.
    B A performance is only worthwhile if the audience is deeply moved.
    C It is essential to learn from one's mistakes.
    D It is necessary to reveal oneself in one's playing.

17 What danger does Little see in becoming much more widely known?

    A She may lose touch with her present audiences.
    B She may have less choice as to the music she can perform.
    C She may find it difficult to cope with the competition.
    D She may be subject to unbearable pressures.

18 Why is Little proud of her latest recording?

    A She did not give way to physical pain during the recording session.
    B The music is particularly challenging to play well.
    C She feels it is a significant musical achievement.
    D The experience has helped her musical development.

19 She feels that listening to recordings of herself is

    A useful.
    B embarrassing.
    C reassuring.
    D exciting.

Remember to put your answers on the separate answer sheet.

THIRD TEXT / QUESTIONS 20–24

*Read this magazine article, then choose the best paragraph from **A–F** to fill each gap **20–24**. There is one extra paragraph which does not belong in any of the gaps.*

MY BIGGEST MISTAKE

My biggest mistake was allowing the debts of one of our distributors to get out of control.

It was shortly after I was promoted to managing director. We were pushing for growth and these particular distributors appeared to be doing a very good job for us in activating the market.

20

The first sign that all was not well was when we began to get slight delays in payments. What used to be a monthly payment was now split into two, three or even four, with the odd little excuses here and there.

21

However, as the new MD, I was so determined Acorn was going to grow that I only heard what I wanted to hear. I accepted that it was a temporary blip, that the mar-ket had been slow for a month or two but that things were looking up. In fact, the distributors were over-stretching themselves. Like many others, they were under-capitalised, relying on a constantly growing volume to finance the business.

22

Eventually we put in place a plan to reel that debt back in, but I should never have allowed things to go that far in the first place.

23

Olivetti, our biggest shareholder, was very supportive, but it was embarrassing – there is no doubt about that.

24

This meant that instead of looking hard at the facts, I looked at the promises of the future. We have potentially been in the same situation several times since, but learned a lot from that mistake.

A With the first impact of the recession, that slowdown in growth in itself was enough to push their capital resources to near breaking point. The only way they could continue was by owing money to suppliers, and their outstanding debt to us had become uncomfortably high.

B First, never assume that things will get better. I wouldn't go so far as to say we were lucky, but in a strange way that lesson alone allowed me to change my attitude in time for the recession.

C When our distributors finally went out of business, we were forced to pick up the tab. There was a total loss of around £1m, which for a company of Acorn's size was no small loss.

D Looking back, I was focusing so hard on the growth in sales that I was hoping to achieve that I forgot my basic financial training.

E We had worked closely with them for several years and they were very dedicated to our product, hence we were their biggest supplier.

F I had full knowledge of these distributors from my experience as sales director and, with my background in finance, I should have been a good deal more cautious.

Remember to put your answers on the separate answer sheet.

FOURTH TEXT / QUESTIONS 25–37

For questions 25–37 match these statements with the descriptions A–F in the magazine article which follows. Some of the descriptions apply to more than one of the statements.

The writer felt nervous on arriving at the health farm.	25 ....
This health farm is very concerned with the guests' attitudes to their own health.	26 ....
You can take part in gentle or energetic fitness training.	27 ....
The swimming pool doesn't suit the needs of some guests.	28 ....
The writer's attitude to being healthy changed during his/her time at the health farm.	29 ....
The publicity material for this health farm does not give a clear impression of the place.	30 ....
The staff know their jobs well.	31 ....
	32 ....
	33 ....
There is no really strenuous exercise here.	34 ....
The food gave cause for complaint.	35 ....
	36 ....
	37 ....

Remember to put your answers on the separate answer sheet.

HEALTH FARM SURVEY

There is still only one place you can go to really get away from it all – a health farm. Facilities include the latest spa treatments, stress-management classes and therapies. To find out exactly how beneficial a health farm can be, we sent six volunteers – each in need of a real break due to bereavement, illness, redundancy or overwork – to test facilities around Britain.

A
Grayshott Hall
Sallie Gibb, 37
Reason for going: *extremely run down, from managing an elderly people's home.*

'At Grayshott Hall I had the warm, welcoming feeling of being a weekend house guest without ever seeing the host.

'Their holistic approach to life encourages you to look after the whole person, the spiritual as well as the physical. I had three consultations during my stay, which helped to highlight how important it is to take time out for ourselves and organise our lives more constructively to prevent our jobs from engulfing us completely.

'Most guests wander around in bathrobes and it is casual, even in the evening. The staff are all extremely friendly, enthusiastic and in plentiful supply.

'There is a choice of two dining rooms: The Greenhouse,

which is the diet room, and The Lakeside Room, and all meals have calorie notes. The food seemed to suit everyone; the only criticism was that the same size portions were served to all, so men complained that there wasn't enough "bulk".

'The treatments are superb and expertly carried out.

'I particularly liked the beautiful indoor pool, which is large and overlooks the gardens and grounds, and never has more than one or two people in it.

'I have been recommending Grayshott to everybody. Four days felt like a fortnight's holiday.'

Grayshott Hall and Health Spa, Grayshott, Nr Hindhead, Surrey GU26 6JJ (0428-604331).

B

Hoar Cross Hall
Jonathan Hardy, 29

Reason for going: *recuperating from a recent operation.*

'Set in the open countryside, with attractive gardens and country lanes, Hoar Cross Hall is an old stately home that has recently been turned into a health spa, incorporating all the latest thalassotherapy treatments.

'I had a wonderfully relaxing back massage, combining aromatherapy oils with infra-red treatment. I felt as if I was walking on air – a fabulous experience. This was followed by a Facial For Men, a face, neck and shoulder massage that uses fabulous-smelling products containing honey, lime and mint. All the staff at the spa were friendly and always smiling.

'The pool is in a lovely setting with water fountains. Great to relax in, but its odd shape makes swimming lengths difficult – and it always has people in it. Breakfast and lunch of fruit and salads were served beside the pool.

'Dinner, however, was less enjoyable. The food was usually either over or under-cooked.

'My main criticism, however, is misleading information in the brochure. Attached to this beautiful, old building is a very modern complex where the vast proportion of bedrooms are – they are not in the grand, old house as you are led to believe.'

Hoar Cross Hall Health Spa, Hoar Cross, Nr Yoxall, Staffordshire DE13 8QS (028-375671).

C

Shrubland Hall
Gill Norman, 55

Reason for going: *suffering from stress, due to work and family worries.*

'From its magnificent surroundings and antiques, to the superb array of therapies and beauty treatments and the homely atmosphere, Shrubland is heaven.

'Nothing is too much trouble; everything is gentle.

'Shrubland offers a wide range of health and beauty treatments. All the therapists are very experienced, which instantly makes you feel relaxed.

'I particularly enjoyed the water therapy treatments, which I really feel I benefited from – particularly the Body

Blitz. Unfortunately, slightly high blood pressure meant I couldn't enjoy any complimentary heat treatments or an aromatherapy massage, so I indulged in a few beauty treatments to make up for it.

'The best thing was the food. I felt completely satisfied; it was exquisitely prepared and tasted wonderful too.'

Shrubland Hall Health Clinic, Coddenham, Ipswich, Suffolk IP6 9QH (0473-830404).

D

Ragdale Hall
Deirdre Farrowes, 64

Reason for going: *suffers from rheumatoid arthritis and thought a health farm may be beneficial for this condition.*

'Ragdale Hall Health Hydro is a straightforward, unpretentious place. The surroundings are lovely.

'I thoroughly enjoyed the complete rest. The day's programme was well organised, with a wide variety of activities on offer and competent staff.

'The treatment facilities are superb, and include a flotation tank, blitz bath and other water treatments, plus a make-up studio. The gymnasium is very well equipped and exercise classes succeed in accommodating all levels of fitness, from stretch-based routines to the more advanced Step Class, which was exhausting even to watch.

'I will definitely recommend Ragdale Hall to my family and friends, and would like to go back for another visit. My only real criticism is that I think the meals could be improved upon

– the evening meal, in particular, was always disappointing.'
Ragdale Hall Health Hydro, Ragdale Village, Nr Melton Mowbray, Leicestershire LE14 3PB (0664-434831).

E
Cedar Falls
Helen Holgate, 34

Reason for going: *made redundant for the second time in a six-month period.*

'As I had never stayed at a health farm before, I was a little apprehensive at first. However, my fears were shortlived:

Cedar Falls has such a relaxing, friendly atmosphere, created by staff and guests, and everything is done for you.

'The range of beauty treatments on offer is excellent, but it is not the place for taxing fitness routines. The gym is basic and exercise routines gentle – they teach exercises that can be done at home without special equipment.

'I enjoyed the food – a light diet menu or haute cuisine (a dietitian will happily make up a menu of 250 calories just for you). On the first day, they recommend a 24-hour fast or

cleansing diet. This gave me such an appetite it's probably the reason I didn't lose any weight!'
Cedar Falls Health Farm, Bishops Lydeard, Taunton, Somerset TA4 3HR (0823-433233).

F
Forest Mere
Jan Newman, 45

Reason for going: *bereavement.*
'The peace and tranquillity of Forest Mere, coupled with being able to switch off completely and let someone else pander to my every need, was sheer heaven.

'The excellent beauty treatments are given by experienced staff in warm rooms. Yoga and dance classes take place in half-lit rooms with soft music and comfortable mats.

'All my meals were very satisfying and well-timed, so I never felt the urge to nibble.

'When I arrived, I was so stressed even my arms and legs were aching, yet after just four days I felt incredibly relaxed. I now have a different outlook and will make more time for myself and my body from now on.'
Forest Mere, Liphook, Hampshire GU30 7JQ (0428-722051).

Cedar Falls

PAPER 2 WRITING (2 hours)

This paper contains one Section A task and four Section B tasks. You must complete the Section A task and one task from Section B.

SECTION A

1 You and your family have just returned from a holiday in England. You spent part of your time at the Royal Bridge Hotel, Merrinmouth. An Australian friend stayed there with you as your guest. The week in Merrinmouth proved to be a disappointment. Look at the hotel brochure and the notes you made on it, and at the hotel notice-board, then write the letters listed below, **using the information given**.

The Royal Bridge Hotel
MERRINMOUTH

You can understand the reluctance of many of our guests to venture far from the elegant charm of the Royal Bridge Hotel – they can see the sweeping bay of sunny Merrinmouth and its many attractions from the secluded grounds as they eat in the Garden Restaurant and attend dinner dances and barbecues.

An energetic programme within the hotel includes Saturday night dances, poolside barbecues and discos. Guests can work out in Stingo's Health Club under professional supervision. The Royal Bridge also employs a children's hostess who plans various activities to keep kids amused during the day. All generations are welcomed and, because of the range of entertainment offered, guests do tend to spend time at the hotel.

'Lunch times are particularly busy,' says general manager, Edwin Rouse. 'People eat and relax in the garden by the pool. The atmosphere evokes a perfect English summer, as guests relax on the sheltered lawn.'

Other holidaymakers, making the most of Merrinmouth's beaches, gardens, theatres and activities, explore the quaint winding streets of the old town, play golf at the premier 18-hole course at Grinham Hall, or perhaps go trout-fishing in the river Merrin, or even have a go at hot-air ballooning, all of which are available nearby.

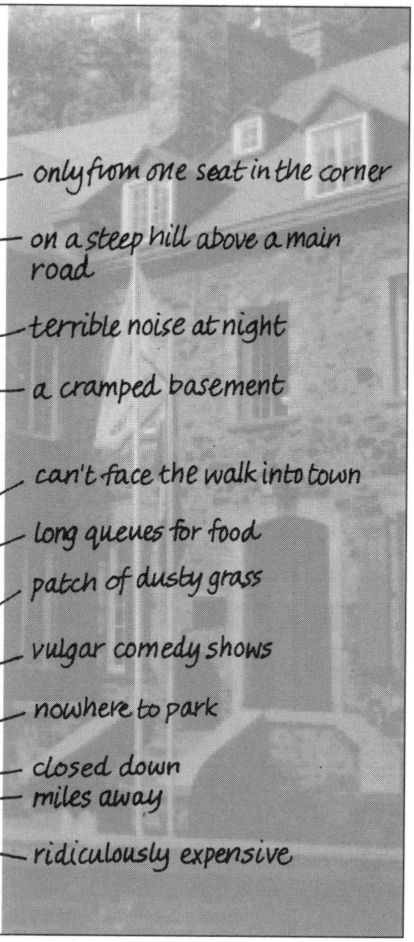

Handwritten notes:
- *only from one seat in the corner*
- *on a steep hill above a main road*
- *terrible noise at night*
- *a cramped basement*
- *can't face the walk into town*
- *long queues for food*
- *patch of dusty grass*
- *vulgar comedy shows*
- *nowhere to park*
- *closed down*
- *miles away*
- *ridiculously expensive*

Royal Bridge Hotel

TODAY'S NOTICES

BREAKFAST 7-9 in the main dining-room
LIGHT LUNCHES are served from the Garden
    Restaurant buffet from 12.30-1.30.
DINNER 8-10 in the main dining-room.
CHILDREN'S HIGH TEAS available in the main
    dining-room 5.30-6.30.

WE REGRET THAT OWING TO ILLNESS, THE CHILDREN'S HOSTESS WILL NOT BE ON DUTY THIS WEEKEND.

WE REGRET THAT THE POOL WILL BE CLOSED FOR SAFETY CHECKS WED-THURS THIS WEEK.

Now write

(a) a **letter** to the travel agent who handled your hotel booking, asking for compensation and explaining why (about 175 words)

(b) a **letter** to your Australian friend apologising for the disappointing holiday (about 75 words)

You must set them out in an appropriate way but it is not necessary to include addresses.

SECTION B

*Choose **ONE** of the following writing tasks. Your answer should follow exactly the instructions given. You are advised to write approximately 250 words.*

2 You have been invited to contribute to an information booklet for foreign visitors to your region, who may be tourists or people coming to live and work there. Write **a section of the booklet** entitled 'Shopping and services'.

3 You have just received the following note from the ten-year-old daughter of some American friends:

> Hi there!
> Thanks very much for the post card. You have some great scenery in your country. Right now, we're studying about the environment in school, and our teacher said we should think about the global environment and how all the different countries have some problems the same and some different. Could you write me about environmental issues in your country? I'd appreciate it, and my teacher would be real impressed.
> With love,
> Debra

Write **a reply** to your young friend.

4 You and your family are going to live abroad for two years and you are going to rent out your home while you are away. You have decided to do this through an international letting agency. Write **a detailed description** of your home for the agency to show potential tenants.

5 You decide to go in for this competition which you see advertised in a travel magazine. Write **your entry**.

WIN ***THE HOLIDAY OF YOUR DREAMS!***

All you have to do is write a description of a really unusual holiday, telling us why you enjoyed it.

We will publish the best entries in our December issue and the winner will receive vouchers worth **£2,000** to spend on the holiday of their choice.

Send your entry to: *Sunway Travel, Competition, Holiday Choices, New Road, Gorston, Kent ME5 8RJ*, not later than May 15th.

Don't forget to label your entry clearly with your name and address.

PAPER 3 ENGLISH IN USE (1 hour 30 minutes)

Answer all questions.

SECTION A

1   *For questions **1–15**, read the text below and decide which word below and on page 101 best fits each space. Put the letter you choose for each question in the correct box on your answer sheet. The exercise begins with an example (0).*

BOOKS BEFORE SCHOOL?

Many parents believe that they should begin to teach their children to read when they are **(0)** ... more than toddlers. This is fine if the child shows a real interest but **(1)** ... a child could be counter-productive if she isn't ready. Wise parents will have a **(2)** ... attitude and take the lead from their child. What they should provide is a selection of **(3)** ... toys, books and other activities. Nowadays there is plenty of good **(4)** ... available for young children, and of course, seeing plenty of books in use about the house will also **(5)** ... them to read.

Of course, books are no longer the only **(6)** ... of stories and information. There is also a huge range of videos, which can **(7)** ... and extend the pleasure a child finds in a book and are **(8)** ... valuable in helping to increase vocabulary and concentration. Television gets a bad **(9)** ... as far as children are concerned, mainly because too many spend too much time watching programmes not intended for their age **(10)** ... . Too many television programmes **(11)** ... an incurious, uncritical attitude that is going to make learning much more difficult. However, **(12)** ... viewing of programmes designed for young children can be useful. Just as adults enjoy reading a book after seeing it **(13)** ... on television, so children will pounce on books which **(14)** ... their favourite television characters, and videos can add a new **(15)** ... to a story known from a book.

0	**A** scarcely	**B** rarely	**C** slightly	**D** really
1	**A** insisting	**B** forcing	**C** making	**D** starting
2	**A** cheerful	**B** contented	**C** relaxed	**D** hopeful
3	**A** bright	**B** thrilling	**C** energetic	**D** stimulating
4	**A** material	**B** sense	**C** produce	**D** amusement
5	**A** provoke	**B** encourage	**C** provide	**D** attract
6	**A** source	**B** site	**C** style	**D** basis
7	**A** uphold	**B** found	**C** reinforce	**D** assist

8	**A** properly	**B** worthily	**C** perfectly	**D** equally
9	**A** review	**B** press	**C** criticism	**D** result
10	**A** set	**B** band	**C** group	**D** limit
11	**A** induce	**B** imply	**C** suggest	**D** attract
12	**A** cautious	**B** choice	**C** approved	**D** discriminating
13	**A** serialised	**B** transferred	**C** revised	**D** visualised
14	**A** illustrate	**B** extend	**C** feature	**D** possess
15	**A** revival	**B** dimension	**C** option	**D** existence

Do not forget to put your answers on the answer sheet.

Example:

2 *For questions **16–30**, complete the following text by writing each missing word on your answer sheet. **Use only one word for each space**. The exercise begins with an example **(0)**.*

PARACHUTING

On the face of it parachuting appears to be a highly risky pastime, **(0)** ... accidents are extremely rare and malfunctions **(16)** ... rarer. Nonetheless, it is a good idea **(17)** ... consider the possible risks before **(18)** ... go. The last place for such thoughts is 600 metres **(19)** ... , hanging out of an open doorway. It is also very important to decide **(20)** ... you are going to be able to cope with the training, both mental and physical. People with an aversion to discipline, for example, might have difficulties **(21)** ... it. At the start of any course you will certainly have to fill in one **(22)** ... more indemnity forms. The style can vary but the message is always the **(23)** ... : If you hurt yourself it's your own stupid fault and **(24)** ... the club's. **(25)** ... clubs may insist that you have a medical before joining the course, **(26)** ... others provide forms where you have to describe the state of your own health. It is **(27)** ... checking before you go just **(28)** ... the club's physical requirements are. In any case you will be very lucky to escape **(29)** ... a few aches and pains, most of **(30)** ... will be accumulated during training.

Do not forget to put your answers on the answer sheet.

Example:

SECTION B

3   *In **most** lines of the following text, there is **one** extra word which is incorrect for reasons either of **grammar or meaning**. For each numbered line **31–42**, write the extra word in the space on your answer sheet.*

Some lines are correct. Indicate these lines with a tick (✓). The exercise begins with three examples (0).

OPERA AND THE ENGLISH

0	When I told an architect friend that I was writing a brief book on opera,
0	he asked if it would tell him 'what he was missing'. The feeling of that he
0	was missing something was a step in the exactly right direction, but the
31	fact that he had lived in England for 45 years without setting his foot in
32	the theatre for an opera performance was a reflection on the small part
33	that opera plays in the lives of the majority of so intelligent people in
34	Britain. The basic appeal of opera is to the heart, if not the head, and the
35	British find the outpouring of emotion and passionate melody feel a little
36	embarrassing. Unlike for the Italians, the Germans and the French, the British
37	have no native operatic tradition of long standing, and so this opera has
38	remained a largely suspect foreign import, which indulged in by the rich, and
39	condemned by intellectuals on the old premise that 'anything too silly
40	to be said, could be sung'. Opera is not really something like that at all.
41	The half of its origins may be aristocratic, but the other half are firmly rooted
42	in the songs, stories and dances of such popular entertainment through the
	centuries.

Do not forget to put your answers on the answer sheet.

Example:

0	✓	0
0	of	0
0	exactly	0

4   *For questions **43–56**, read the following statement made by Barbara Bailey after witnessing a road accident and use the information to complete the numbered gaps in the letter to her sister. Then write the new words in the correct spaces on your answer sheet. **Use no more than two words** for each gap. The exercise begins with an example (0). The words you need **do not occur** in the notes.*

WITNESS STATEMENT: Barbara Bailey
Date: 23/3/94

On Tuesday, 20th March, 1994, I was driving home at
approximately 7 p.m., after working late at my office in Park
Street. I decided to use the ring road in order to avoid the
traffic jams in the vicinity of the sports stadium. Although
the traffic was rather heavy, it was moving quite freely. As I
approached London Road corner, I was overtaken by a red sports
car, in spite of the fact that the traffic lights were red. A
few minutes later I saw the car at the roundabout. The driver
pulled on to the roundabout in the path of a van. It was
clearly impossible for the van driver to stop in time to avoid
hitting the car, which was spun round. In my opinion, the car
driver was very lucky not to be injured, considering how badly
his car was damaged. The only damage to the van, as far as I
am aware, was that the headlights were smashed.

LETTER

Dear Sheila,

*Just a note to reassure you that I'm all right – I was only a witness to the accident I
mentioned on the phone!*

*It was last Tuesday, as I was on my way home from work. It was (0) ... for
sevenish, I think. I'd been doing (43) ... again! I thought it'd be a (44) ... to use the ring
road because I (45) ... to get stuck in the jams (46) ... the Stadium. There was a fair
(47) ... traffic but it was moving OK.*

*Well, you know the corner of London Road? I was (48) ... to the traffic lights when
this red sports car shot past me, (49) ... the lights were (50) ... him. When I got to
the roundabout I spotted him again. He pulled out in front of a van. The van driver
had (51) ... of stopping in time, and he went straight into the car. It turned the car
round in (52) ... . I reckon the driver (53) ... lightly as he wasn't hurt at all (54) ... his
car was a real mess. Fortunately, the van was still in one (55) ..., at least I think so,
(56) ... the headlights, which were smashed, of course.*

*Anyway, none of it involved me – I just had to hang about and make a statement –
so don't worry!*

Lots of love,
Barbara

Do not forget to put your answers on the answer sheet.

Example:

0	getting on	0

SECTION C

5 *For questions **57–63**, read through the following text and then choose from list **A–K** the best phrase or sentence given below it to fill each of the blanks. Write one letter (**A–K**) in the correct box on your answer sheet. **Some of the suggested answers do not fit at all.** One answer has been given as an example (**0**).*

THE LANGUAGE OF CLOTHES – PATTERN AND DECORATION

From a utilitarian point of view there is no need for clothes to be decorated with trimming or embroidery, **(0)** ... . Since these elaborations add needlessly to the cost of garments, **(57)** ... . As a rule, the more complex the design, and the more colours used, **(58)** ... of the garment. It is also true, however, that a plain-coloured material shows marks **(59)** ... , and once weaving and machine-printing had made patterned fabrics relatively inexpensive **(60)** ... . Today there is not much difference in prestige between patterned and plain, **(61)** ... . Clothes that have obviously been decorated **(62)** ... (usually by embroidery or appliqué) continue to be excellent advertisements for conspicuous consumption. **(63)** ... that combine large areas of pale, easily soiled plain fabric with elaborate hand decoration.

A   no longer a matter of social status

B   the greater the prestige

C   they have always tended to confer status

D   more readily than a patterned one

E   without paying attention to fashion

F   Most prestigious of all are those garments

G   unless the design is hand-printed

H   after they were assembled

I   The high cost of clothes

J   their status somewhat declined

K   or to be made of patterned fabrics

Do not forget to put your answers on the answer sheet.

Example:

104

6 *Use the following notes to write out a description of the Staffordshire Potteries to be included in a tour brochure. Write* **one complete sentence** *on the answer sheet for each numbered set of notes, using connecting words and phrases as appropriate. You may add words and change the form of the words given in the notes but do not add any extra information. The first point has been expanded for you as an example* **(0).**

THE STAFFORDSHIRE POTTERIES

0	N. Staffs ideal place potteries: natural resources – clay, coal, water
81	Evidence pottery industry 14th century
82	17th century most produce → local use
83	Tea drinking (new fashion) → more demand cups etc
84	18th century: development refined pottery by Staffs potters e.g. Wedgwood & Spode
85	Designs: influence of recent excavations (Italy) & imports (China)
86	Same time, canals = improved communications, Staffs pottery → abroad
87	Nowadays, Staffs pottery still popular → high prices, antiques auctions

---

The space below can be used for your rough answers.
Do not forget to put your answers on the answer sheet.

0	North Staffordshire was an ideal place for the potteries, with its natural resources of clay, coal and water.
81	
82	
83	
84	
85	
86	
87	

PAPER 4 LISTENING (45 minutes)

Answer all questions.

SECTION A

*For questions **1–10** you will hear a student telling her class about Henry Ford, the inventor. As you listen, complete the information in the notes.*

You will hear the recording twice.

Henry Ford

b. 1863 on farm in [_____ **1**] USA.

When young learnt about machinery by [_____ **2**]

Married young.

First experiments inspired by sight of [_____ **3**]

At that time vehicle motors usually [_____ **4**] or electric.

Got job with Edison Electric Co.

Worked at night in his [_____ **5**]

1883 wife helped to get first engine going in [_____ **6**]

1896 drove first vehicle: Quadricycle.

1898 second car.

1901 Began racing in order to [_____ **7**]

Achieved speed of 44.8 m.p.h.

V. dangerous because he was sitting on top of [_____ **8**]

1904 set new world speed record at track across [_____ **9**]

Speed was [_____ **10**] m.p.h.

SECTION B

You will hear a man confirming details of a business trip to China for his boss.
For questions **11–17** *complete the schedule for the trip.*

Listen very carefully as you will hear this piece only ONCE.

China trip — Dr Margaret Green

Tues: evening arrive Shanghai airport, to be met by Mr Liu, (the)
        [_____|**11**] & taken to Peace Hotel

Wed: 10am: meeting at University [_____|**12**] Dept.
        Transport to be organised by [_____|**13**]
        Lunch with [_____|**14**] Committee.
        pm: museum visit (Mr Liu) to see [_____|**15**]
        and paintings

Thur: 8am: depart hotel with Mr Liu for day in
        [_____|**16**] industrial area.

Fri: Shopping at [_____|**17**] near hotel.
        11am: taxi from hotel to airport.

SECTION C

You will hear an excerpt from a radio programme, 'Business Matters', in which Shirley, a woman whose business partner disappeared with all their money, discusses her experiences. For questions 18–22 you must choose the best answer A, B, C or D.

You will hear the piece twice.

18 How did Shirley feel when she discovered that her partner had taken her money?

    A in despair
    B betrayed
    C furious
    D disgusted

19 When she told her lawyer, he was

    A indifferent.
    B calm.
    C puzzled.
    D shocked.

20 Who gave her the most support?

    A her husband
    B her daughter
    C her doctor
    D her neighbour

21 The address of her former partner is

    A completely unknown.
    B known to the police.
    C false.
    D probably quite near.

22 What does Shirley plan to do?

    A retire for the sake of her health
    B find employment
    C start a business with her husband
    D train for a new career

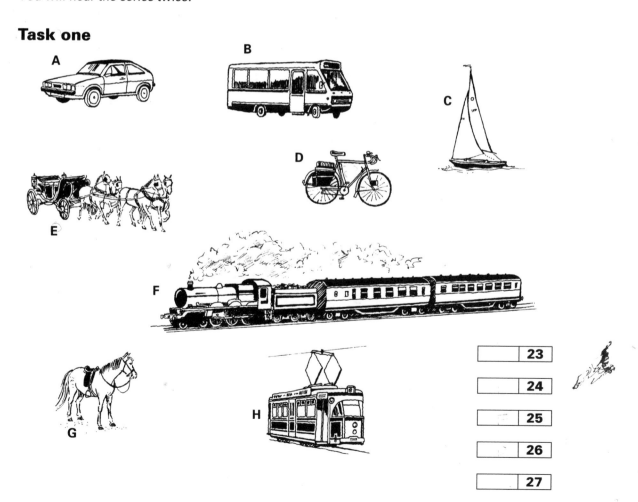

SECTION D

You will hear extracts of five different people talking. They are all talking about some kind of journey.

Task one

*Pictures **A–H** show various different forms of transport. As you listen, put them in order by completing the boxes numbered **23–27** with the appropriate letter.*

Task two

*Letters **A–H** list the different feelings described by the people speaking in the extracts. As you listen, put them in order by completing the boxes numbered **28–32** with the appropriate letter.*

You will hear the series twice.

Task one

A

B

C

D

E

F

G

H

	23
	24
	25
	26
	27

Task two

A   exhaustion

B   relaxation

C   irritation

D   amusement

E   excitement

F   anger

G   discomfort

H   fear

	28
	29
	30
	31
	32

Note: For Paper 5 see pages **149–150** and the Colour Section.

Part 3   The Key

Practice Test 1

PAPER 1   READING   (1 hour 15 minutes)

First text: 1 E   2 J (1 and 2 interchangeable)
3 F   4 G   5 I (3, 4 and 5 interchangeable)
6 H   7 I   8 G   9 A   10 C   11 B   12 D
13 G   14 D   15 J   16 B   17 C   18 E   19 F

Second text: 20 B   21 D   22 A   23 D   24 C   25 C

Third text: 26 E   27 A   28 D   29 G   30 C   31 F

Fourth text: 32 F
33 B   34 F   35 G (33, 34 and 35 interchangeable)
36 C   37 C   38 D   39 E   40 A   41 F   42 H
43 D   44 F   45 A

PAPER 2   WRITING

Section A   Plan

1a <u>letter</u> to Acme Agents (business)
want to book 15 tickets
date, place
pay on night?
discount?
finishing time?

1b <u>letter</u> to Mr and Mrs Andersen (tactful, friendly)
sorry they're annoyed
not a question of language level
type of production – violence
special effects frightening?
nb other event for kids (?invent e.g.)

1c <u>note</u> to Sam (friendly, informal)
have written to book & check about paying & length
have written to A.s as asked - hope for best (give copy later?)

Section A   *Model answers*

1a

12th March, 19..

Dear Sir or Madam,

I am the secretary of the International Friendship Club, here in Perth. We would like to book 15 seats for Macbeth here on Saturday, 16th May.

I understand that we may pay in dollars on the night of the performance and that the charge for a group will be the equivalent of £6 per person. Could you confirm that we will get the group discount if we do not pay in advance?

Please could you also let me know what time the play will end (I believe it starts at 8 pm) ?

Thank you for your help.

Yours sincerely,

Andreas Peto

ANDREAS PETO
Club Secretary

1b

12th March, 19..

Dear Mr and Mrs Andersen,

I am writing on behalf of the Club committee to explain the decision not to buy tickets for your children for Macbeth. We're very sorry that you're annoyed by this. We know that your children speak very good English, but we believe that this production is really only for adults. It shows very realistic violence and the special effects are used in a scene which is said to be genuinely frightening.

We hope you are not too disappointed and that the children will continue to enjoy our events for younger members, such as the Fancy Dress Party next weekend.

With best wishes,

Andreas Peto

ANDREAS PETO
Club Secretary

1c

12th March

Dear Sam,

I've written to Acme Productions to book 15 seats and checked about price etc. as you asked. I've also written to the Andersens, which was pretty difficult actually. Let's hope they accept our decision now. I'll let you have a copy of my letter when we meet.

All the best,

Andreas

Section B Plans

---

2 (magazine <u>article</u>, fairly informal)
¶ 1 many people: best way = go to Eng.
       but 1 – expensive
           2 – lonely?
¶ 2 my opinion – most imp. thing = teacher + student
       compare old school / present one
¶ 3 using my Eng. – enjoyable
       my advice: find good class teacher and enjoy

---

3 (<u>letter</u>, friendly, informal)
¶ 1 sympathy, hope not too bored etc. Everyone misses her . . .
¶ 2 horrible journey: traffic jams, missed turning (Paulina's map-reading), arrived v. late, cottage owner angry
¶ 3 lovely place, weather not bad, storm today (time to write)
¶ 4 sightseeing tomorrow – ancient ruins, eating out (Alan's terrible cooking)
¶ 5 OK, but miss her. Not again without her (Alan & Paulina argue). Go somewhere on our own at end of summer?

---

4 (<u>guidebook</u>, friendly, not too informal)
¶ 1 Not great entertainment centre, but still something for most ages & prices
¶ 2 Conventional theatre – small town, visiting companies, some amateur, variety of shows e.g. mod. drama, dance etc. Phone no, address, approx price
¶ 3 Karaoke – local hotel, mostly English songs, students & teenagers, free before 9 pm, charges later, address
¶ 4 Folk dance displays – dates & venues at town hall. Most villages during summer

---

5 *(business <u>letter</u>)*
¶ 1 age, college etc. (Why I want English)
¶ 2 grandparents' farm – helping since young, typical jobs
¶ 3 like children, look after younger brothers, enjoy sports
¶ 4 not enjoy housework but can do
¶ 5 driving test next month
¶ 6 easy-going, enjoy life, esp. outdoors
¶ 7 ref available

Section B   Model answers

2

Many people say that the best way to learn English is to go to England. Being with people who do not speak your language forces you to use English to communicate and many students find that this is the best way to gain confidence. However, there are two disadvantages. First, it is very expensive. Second, it can be quite lonely especially if you know very little English. If you are not used to looking after yourself, this may not be the way for you.

In my opinion, the most important aspect of language learning is the relationship between the student and the teacher. If the student trusts the teacher and is willing to work hard, he or she will learn a lot. At my last school, I had little faith in my teachers, because they were poorly trained and simply followed the exercises in a course book. Now I go to a school where the teachers make us want to work because the classes are so interesting. We have lots of homework and sometimes it's quite hard, but it's fun as well, so we don't mind.

I already use my English to enjoy films and rock music and to talk to foreign visitors to my country. I enjoy these conversations and I think they are just as useful as expensive private lessons. My advice to anyone who wants to learn a foreign language is to find a class with a teacher who motivates you – and then enjoy yourself!

3

Dear Sara,

We were really sorry you couldn't come with us. I do hope you're not too bored, sitting at home with your leg in plaster. You certainly didn't miss any fun on the journey. There were terrible traffic jams, which meant we spent hours looking at the back of the car in front. Then, when we did move, we missed the turning off the motorway – that was Paulina's fault, she can't read a map properly and she wouldn't let me help. We were extremely late getting to the cottage and the owner had been waiting to let us in and was very angry.

It is a lovely place though! We can see the sea from the garden and the countryside is very pretty. The weather has been quite good – up to today, anyway. At the moment there is a storm with gale force winds and icy rain! This explains how I have time to write such a long letter.

We plan to go sightseeing tomorrow round some of the ancient ruins. And we're going to eat out in a restaurant to give us a break from Alan's cooking, which is terrible. Even worse than mine!

Apart from that we're OK. I do miss you though. I won't come away with Alan and Paulina again without you. They argue almost all the time, which makes me so tense. If I could get another week off, would you like us to go somewhere on our own at the end of the summer?

Lots of love,
        Laurie

4

Live entertainment in Westsee

Although Westsee is known more for its elegant nineteenth century architecture than its night-life, it can offer a good range of entertainment. There is something for all ages and to suit most budgets. Here are some of the events you might like to know about:

The New Theatre Market Place, Westsee
This comfortable little theatre, built in the 1950s, offers a variety of shows, including modern drama, dance and other performances, both by visiting professional companies and by some excellent local amateur groups. Prices from £10.50 (concessions for students). Tel: 20566 for programme details and bookings. Box office open 10 am – 8 pm weekdays.

Karaoke at the Bear Hotel, Bridge Street
Friday and Saturday nights in the Club Room from 8 pm – 11 pm. This is popular with local teenagers and students, who make visitors feel very welcome. Most of the songs are in English. Prizes every evening. Entrance free before 9 pm, charge of £3.50 per person after that.

Folk dance
Throughout the summer (June – September) local folk dance clubs give displays in most village squares and some public gardens in the area. Beautiful traditional costumes are worn and both the dancing and the music are of a very high standard. Well worth seeing. No charge is made but a collection is taken to cover costs. Performances are usually on Wednesday evenings and Saturday afternoons. A list of dates and venues is available from the information office at the Town Hall.

via Garibaldi 15
Villafranca
18 / 5 / ..

H. Daunce
Fullers Farm
Little Cote
Nr Salisbury
Wilts, UK

Dear Mr Daunce,

I have seen your advertisement for help during July and August and I am very interested in the job you offer. I am nineteen years old, I live in Villafranca in Italy and I am planning to study English at University , so two months in England would be just the thing for me. I think I have most of the qualifications you require.

My grandparents have a small farm and I have spent many weeks helping them during school holidays, so I am used to working outdoors. I usually help at harvest time and often drive the tractor and help to repair buildings etc.

I have two younger brothers and I have helped to look after them since they were little. They are now aged twelve and fourteen. I am quite keen on sports myself, especially swimming and volleyball.

I have to admit that I do not enjoy housework, but I have had plenty of practice, so I can do it quite well.

I am taking my driving test next month and I expect to pass.

I think I am an easy-going person as I get on well with most people, even my little brothers! I enjoy life and have lots of friends and I think I have a good sense of humour. I like being outdoors and being active.

My teacher has said he would be willing to give me a character reference if you wish.

I hope you will consider my application and I look forward to hearing from you.

Yours sincerely,

Anna Maria Bianchi
ANNA MARIA BIANCHI

PAPER 3 ENGLISH IN USE   (1 hour 30 minutes)

Section A

Question 1   [One mark for each correct answer]

1 A   2 B   3 C   4 D   5 A   6 B   7 C   8 D   9 A   10 A
11 B   12 C   13 D   14 A   15 C

Question 2   [One mark for each correct answer]

16 are   17 in/when/before   18 is   19 Otherwise   20 the
21 this/so   22 substitute/replacement   23 with   24 else   25 itself
26 not   27 that/this   28 it   29 can/may   30 or

Section B

Question 3   [One mark for each correct answer]

31 Principle   32 √   33 distinction   34 √   35 exciting
36 pieces   37 √   38 Experience   39 development   40 further
41 indivisible   42 already   43 research   44 behaviour

Question 4   [One mark for each correct answer]

45 must/should inform   46 later than   47 only   48 satisfied
49 regard/reference/respect   50 following   51 punctual
52 compulsory   53 completion   54 conditions   55 full
56 written   57 circumstances   58 recommendation

Section C

Question 5   [One mark for each correct answer]

59 G   60 J   61 A   62 D   63 C   64 K   65 I

Question 6   [These are specimen answers – up to two marks for each sentence]

81 A hire car has been booked from Bristows, the garage opposite the station, for which a £25 deposit is payable on collection.
82 From Bristows turn left into Station Road, then follow the Coast Road, which is clearly signed, for 3 km until you reach Ocean Ridge cottage at the top of the hill.
83 The water supply is already connected, but for electricity you need some £1 coins to put in the meter, which is behind the door.
84 The phone in the hall accepts incoming calls only.
85 Please remember to supervise children whenever they use the path from the back garden to the beach as it is very steep, and the cottage owner cannot be held responsible for accidents.
86 Always lock the cottage when you go out because unfortunately there have been frequent thefts from holiday homes recently, resulting in the loss of valuables such as cash, credit cards and cameras.

PAPER 4 LISTENING (45 minutes)

Section A [One mark for each correct answer]

1 famous   2 national   3 origins (and development)
4 (the) Middle Ages   5 (early) industrial machines   6 living conditions
7 Living Memories   8 prints/works

Section B [One mark for each correct answer]

9 National Zoological Society   10 Maria Altrim   11 Open Partnerships
12 Forward Thinking   13 Eastern Land Conservation   14 D(octo)r Scott
15 Land Chemistry   16 Harnessing the Wind

Section C [One mark for each correct answer]

17 J   18 KJ   19 J   20 K   21 N   22 K   23 K   24 J

Section D [One mark for each correct answer]

25 B   26 A   27 G   28 F   29 E   30 E   31 G   32 A   33 C
34 H

Transcript

This is the Certificate in Advanced English, Listening Test. Practice Test number 1. There are four sections to the test, A, B, C and D. You will hear Section B once only. All the other parts of the test will be heard twice. During the test, there will be a pause before each part to allow you to look through the questions, and other pauses to let you think about your answers. At the end of every pause you will hear this sound.

tone

You should write your answers on the question paper. You will have ten minutes at the end to transfer your answers to the separate answer sheet. The tape will now be stopped. You must ask any questions now, as you will not be allowed to speak during the test.

[*pause*]

Section A. You will hear a museum guide welcoming a party of visitors. Look at the notes below and complete the information for questions 1–8 using up to three words in each space. You will hear the recording twice.

[*pause*]

tone

Guide: Good morning everyone and welcome to Lampley and District Museum. Before you go round, I'd just like to tell you a little about how the museum is organised. It was founded twenty-five years ago, and brings together under one roof the contents of the former Lampley Guild Hall collection and the South Welting Gallery. Since its foundation it has received a number of bequests, and also gifts from the local archaeological society. The collection is divided into four sections.
    First of all, we attempt to put Lampley on the national map, so to speak, with

our collection of portraits illustrating some of the city's more famous sons and daughters. There is also, currently, a montage of pictures, photographs and documents concerned with events of national significance, seen in the lives of the people of Lampley.

Having, we hope, whetted your appetites, we then take a longer view of the city. In Section Two, we have first of all a series of maps and cases of exhibits related to the origins and early development of the city, and then next, these lead us into some displays, which are in fact reconstructions and are the work of a local school, and are both extraordinarily detailed and accurate, illustrating life in Lampley in the Middle Ages. I'm sure you will be fascinated by them.

Section Three will be of interest to any of you who like machines, as well as social historians. After a period of relative obscurity, Lampley grew vigorously during the Industrial Revolution, and we have several working models of early machines used in the region's factories. Of course, in the early days, there was a great influx of workers and their families, and although we in Lampley have always prided ourselves on the generally enlightened attitudes of the industrialists in the area, the images in the last part of Section Three does remind us that living conditions were pretty dreadful for industrial workers a hundred and fifty years ago. In Section Four, we have again drawn on the resources of our younger citizens, who have been guided for several years past by our curator in the putting together of a regularly up-dated audio-visual exhibition based entirely on reminiscences and eye-witness accounts of local and national events. It's entitled 'Living Memories' and it's very popular with both old and young visitors.

Lastly, also in Section Four, we have a small collection of works by some of the best artists currently working in the region. With our limited space, we can't represent them all together, so exhibits are renewed monthly. At present Lampley Contemporary Printmakers are having a show, and all the works are for sale. Now I hope you'll enjoy going round the museum and please don't hesitate to ask me if you have any questions. I'll do my best to answer them! Thank you.

[*pause*]

tone

Now you will hear the piece again. [The recording is repeated.]

[*pause*]

That is the end of Section A.

[*pause*]

Section B. You will hear a recording from the telephone answering machine of a conference organiser. As you listen, fill in the information on the booking forms for questions 9–16. Listen very carefully as you will hear this piece only once.

[*pause*]

tone

Answering machine: Thank you for calling the International Conference Centre. This line is for the registration of options at the next conference. If you have any queries please call the information line number in your brochure. To register for options, please leave a message on this line now, stating clearly the name of your organisation, your name, and the options chosen, which should be two in number. Please begin after the tone.

Caller 1: This is ... the National Zoological Society, erm Zoological Society, erm, I am Maria Altrim. That's A-L-T-R-I-M, that's M for mother, Altrim, erm and we would like to register for two optional sessions, erm, first, the one called 'Open Partnerships' which is in the morning, and then after lunch we'd like, erm, to join the discussion group called, erm, 'Forward Thinking'. Erm, that's all.

Caller 2: My name's – oh sorry, my organisation is Eastern – Land – Conservation. And my name is Doctor Scott, that's Scott with a double T, and, er, we'd like to enrol for the sessions called 'Land Chemistry' and 'Harnessing the Wind'. That's 'Land Chemistry' in the morning, and 'Harnessing the Wind' in the afternoon. Um, er, thank you.

[*pause*]

That is the end of Section B.

[*pause*]

Section C. You will hear a radio programme in which a mother, Jane, and a father, Kenneth, discuss whether it is a good idea for young people to take a year out before going to university, to travel around the world. During their discussion they express various views. For questions 17–24, indicate which views are expressed by Jane and Kenneth, by writing J (for Jane) or K (for Kenneth) or N (for neither) in the box provided. You may write both initials if Jane and Kenneth express the same opinion. You will hear the piece twice.

[*pause*]

tone

Kenneth: ... the thing is, as I see it, it's really an opportunity they shouldn't waste, I mean, it's a privilege, even in affluent countries ...

Jane: Well, yes, of course, I'm not saying that university isn't important, it's the age that isn't so crucial, I think. It doesn't matter really whether you're twenty-one or twenty-three or even thirty, a university degree is a university degree, but the chance to go all over the place, to see other countries, other cultures, before you're set in your ways, without a lot of preconceived ideas, prejudices even ...

Kenneth: Mm, well ...

Jane: I think that's what we should see this as. And meeting people.

Kenneth: I don't deny it's good to have friends all round the world, and of course, the younger you are, the easier you make them, you're less inhibited ...

Jane: Well, exactly, it's ideal. And you can afford to be adventurous because you know there's somewhere you can retreat to, somewhere you can run and hide, in your parents' place.

Kenneth: I don't know about that.

Jane: Oh, surely?

Kenneth: I'm not so sure. But I do think, provided they're sensible in what they do, the experience, the knowledge of the world, that's going to stand them in good stead when it comes to prospective employers. They're going to be sounding as if they know a thing or two, give them the edge over the others in the office.

That's where the outlay is going to be justified because, well, after all, it's going to cost a bob or two, isn't it?

Jane: Well, it would if they wanted to do it in luxury, but that's the point, when they're young they can rough it a bit without minding, so they can do it on a tight budget.

Kenneth: I still think I, we, whoever, we're going to end up well out of pocket. You just have to hope it's a worthwhile investment. So, although they may be late starters, have got a bit of catching up to do, career-wise, the boss'll be so taken with their maturity of approach, he ...

Jane: Or she ...

Kenneth: True. Or she, will value them anyway.

Jane: They should learn to use their common sense, if nothing else.

Kenneth: Personally, I think that's something you're born with. No amount of travel, however old or young you are, will give you that!

Jane: Do you really? Well, it's a point of view, I suppose...

[*pause*]

tone

Now you will hear the piece again. [The recording is repeated.]

[*pause*]

That is the end of Section C.

[*pause*]

Now look at Section D for the fourth and last part of the test. You will hear extracts of five different people talking. They are all talking about some kind of meeting. Look at Task One. Letters A–H list various different people. As you listen, put them in order by completing the boxes numbered 25–29 with the appropriate letter. Now look at Task Two. Letters A–H list the different meetings mentioned by the people speaking in the extracts. As you listen, put them in order by completing the boxes numbered 30–34 with the appropriate letter. You will hear the series twice.

[*pause*]

tone

Businessman: Well, I said, I told him, you can't honestly expect me to go through the whole deal here. It was a real hole. Anyway, they soon realised they'd misjudged their man, and sent a limo to whisk me out to company HQ. And I got the red carpet treatment there, no mistake. Met the chairman and the board, and had lunch with them! There's great potential there if we make a quick follow-up.

Mother: You'll have to explain yourself to Dad. You're old enough to make your own apologies. Do you know he waited three-quarters of an hour for you at the bus station, in case you were on the next one. I can tell you he's not at all amused.

Local government official: Now, that's an example of what makes this worthwhile. I've just been round to the hospital, and talked to the contractor. He's a decent chap, like I said, and, er, he saw our point of view. We can't waste taxpayers' money, I said, and he said, fair enough and he'll have the revised documents here by Monday.

Former schoolfriend: It was that new place out near the station, you know? I'd have known her anywhere. There she was, the last person in the world you'd think of running a restaurant. She always came bottom in domestic science! Wouldn't have missed it for the world. Spent much longer than I'd planned of course, but, what the hell, it was such a coincidence. There was so much to catch up on.

Rock star: Somehow I'd thought they'd be different. You get so many idiots, following whatever the papers tell them, you know, whoever's flavour of the month. Well, these guys had been so, I don't know, loyal, whatever, I thought, they'll understand what I'm trying to say to audiences, they'll have thought about what the words mean, you know. But they're just like all the others, it's the glamour that attracts them.

[*pause*]

tone

Now you will hear the piece again. [The recording is repeated.]

[*pause*]

That is the end of Section D. There will now be a ten-minute pause for you to transfer your answers to the separate answer sheet. Be sure to follow the numbering of all the questions. The question papers and answer sheets will then be collected by your supervisor.

[*pause*]

That is the end of the test.

Practice Test 2

PAPER 1 READING   (1 hour 15 minutes)

First text:	1 B	2 D	3 A	(1, 2 and 3 interchangeable)
	4 J	5 G	(4 and 5 interchangeable)	
	6 A	7 C	(6 and 7 interchangeable)	
	8 G	9 H	10 I	(8, 9 and 10 interchangeable)
	11 E	12 F	13 H	

Second text:	14 D	15 D	16 A	17 C	18 B	
Third text:	19 A	20 G	21 E	22 H	23 D	24 F	25 C
Fourth text:	26 H	27 G	28 E	29 D	30 B	31 A
	32 A	33 C	34 A	35 B	36 C	37 G	38 E
	39 F	40 C				

PAPER 2 WRITING

See Study Notes p. 5 for general advice and Practice Test 1 Key p. 111 for sample plans and answers.

PAPER 3 ENGLISH IN USE (1 hour 30 minutes)

Section A

Question 1 [One mark for each correct answer]

1 A   2 D   3 B   4 B   5 A   6 B   7 C   8 A   9 C   10 A
11 B   12 B   13 D   14 B   15 A

Question 2 [One mark for each correct answer]

16 for/when   17 One   18 either/whether   19 is   20 the
21 other   22 many   23 who   24 even/in   25 but   26 the   27 back
28 are   29 to   30 those

Section B

Question 3 [One mark for each correct answer]

31 √   32 case   33 had   34 made   35 seeing   36 √
37 more   38 collectors   39 promising   40 Later   41 sent
42 botanist   43 √

Question 4 [One mark for each correct answer]

44 welcomed/greeted   45 discussion/conversation   46 was shown
47 student accommodation/rooms   48 was provided/prepared
49 praised   50 compared   51 visited two/some   52 his attention
53 condition/state   54 a need/case   55 (every) reason/cause

Section C

Question 5 [One mark for each correct answer]

56 E   57 G   58 H   59 I   60 B   61 A

Question 6 [These are specimen answers – up to two marks for each sentence]

81 I suggest you do a rice salad, which is easy to make and tasty, but not too expensive.
82 All you need is lots of colourful vegetables, like carrots and peppers, and some onion, cut into small chunks, rice, and salad dressing.
83 Using a large, heavy pan, soften the vegetables in oil or butter for five minutes.
84 Add water, rice and salt and cook it until the rice is done.
85 Meanwhile, make a salad dressing by mixing lemon juice or vinegar with oil (olive if you have it), mustard and pepper.
86 Rinse the rice and vegetables in hot water, and then, before they cool, add the dressing, stirring well.
87 This is also very good if you add things like chopped nuts, eggs or cheese at the same time as the dressing.

PAPER 4 LISTENING (45 minutes)

Section A [One mark for each correct answer]

1 New Zealand   2 farm (house)   3 Festival   4 posters   5 printer
6 Late Flowering   7 Hensham Community Centre   8 3–9 August
9 13.45 / 1.45 / quarter to two

Section B [One mark for each correct answer]

10 waterproof   11 hood   12 frame   13 sweets/chocolate
14 cans (of drink)   15 small notebooks   16 envelope

Section C [One mark for each correct answer]

17 R   18 N   19 O   20 R   21 O   22 O   23 R   24 N
25 R   26 O

Section D [One mark for each correct answer]

27 B   28 C   29 A   30 F   31 H   32 A   33 C   34 D
35 F   36 G

Transcript

This is the Certificate in Advanced English, Listening Test. Practice Test number 2. There are four sections to the test, A, B, C and D. You will hear Section B once only. All the other parts of the test will be heard twice. During the test, there will be a pause before each part to allow you to look through the questions, and other pauses to let you think about your answers. At the end of every pause you will hear this sound.

tone

You should write your answers on the question paper. You will have ten minutes at the end to transfer your answers to the separate answer sheet. The tape will now be stopped. You must ask any questions now, as you will not be allowed to speak during the test.

[*pause*]

Section A. Candy Watkins works in the tourist office of a small town in the West of England. Each morning her first job is to check the messages on the telephone answering machine for her boss, Heather. Look at her notes below and complete the information for questions 1–9. You will hear the recording twice.

[*pause*]

tone

V1: [answerphone] This is Hensham Tourist Office. We are sorry there is no one to take your call at the moment. Please leave a message after the tone, or call again during office opening hours, which are 9.30 to 4, Monday to Friday. Thank you.

V2: Oh, eh, this is er, Ed Benkel here. Erm, we'd like, er that is, the wife and I, er, that's Mr and Mrs Benkel, er, we'd like to make a booking through you, er, we're over from New Zealand and we want to stay in Hensham for three nights, er, in bed and breakfast, er, we'd like to stay in a farmhouse, er, not in the town, er, starting Friday. Can you fix that? Er, I'll call you tomorrow to confirm. Thank you.

V3:   Durham here. Monty Durham. Henmouth Festival Office. Right. We've got the posters for the festival. That is, the printer fellow's got 'em. He'll deliver direct to you, save a lot of hassle. So, question is, how many do you want? Okey-dokey? Be in touch.

V4:   Erm, I'm phoning on behalf of Oxbow Players, er, you know, drama group? You very kindly agreed, erm, to publicise our production this summer, so I'm phoning to tell you, erm, about it. Erm, it's called 'Late Flowering', it's a comedy, at least it's supposed to be. We'll be doing it at the usual venue, that's Hensham Community Centre of course, and er, thank you for er – oh, yes, it'll be the third to the ninth of August. Er, thank you very much.

V5:   Erm, Mum? I mean, Candy, can you let Mum, I mean Heather, know that I'll be late? They've changed the time of my driving lesson from half past ten to half past twelve, so I'll get the eleven o'clock bus, but I want a lift home so I'll come to the office at quarter to two, so can you, I mean she, wait for me? Thanks.

[*pause*]

tone

Now you will hear the piece again. [The recording is repeated.]

[*pause*]

That is the end of Section A.

[*pause*]

Section B. You will hear a college tutor giving some information to a group of students about arrangements for a field trip. As you listen, fill in the information on the booking forms for questions 10–16. Listen very carefully as you will hear this piece only once.

[*pause*]

tone

Tutor: Thank you all for coming in. I just want to run through a few details about the field trip at the beginning of next term. It's mainly things you need, I thought perhaps you could get them together over the vacation. Anyway, erm, first of all, yes, clothing. Obviously we'll be in some pretty damp spots, so the most important thing, and this really is a must, is waterproof gear for your feet. It doesn't really matter whether that's gumboots, or climbing boots, or whatever, as long as they don't let the wet in. It's also going to rain some of the time, so can I urge you to find yourself a jacket that has an integral hood? There's nothing more miserable than trying to do research with cold water running down the back of your neck, and really a hood's the only thing. And it can't get lost like a hat can.

Now, bags. I realise you won't all have one, but if you can borrow, or even hire, a backpack which has a frame, you'll save yourself a lot of backache. The frame makes all the difference when you're carrying it some distance.

Then, what else? Oh, yes. A do and a don't. Do fix yourself up with a few packets of sweets. There's nowhere to buy them, and a bar of chocolate or something is a real treat when you're cold and wet and two miles from base. On the other hand, don't bring canned drinks. There is a supply provided, anyway, and cans are much too heavy to carry all that way.

Lastly, just an idea about stationery. The best thing is to bring a couple of fairly small notebooks rather than the sort of big files we usually use. Something that'll go in your pocket. And also, and I expect you've already got something that'll do, bring a clear plastic envelope or something like that to keep the notebooks in. Otherwise you risk losing all your notes to the rain! OK. Any questions about any of that, or the travel arrangements …

[*pause*]

That is the end of Section B.

[*pause*]

Section C. You will hear a discussion between three people, Ray, Nonna and Owen, who are talking about the problems they have in travelling around the city where they live. For questions 17–26, indicate which solutions are proposed by each speaker. Write R for Ray, N for Nonna, or O for Owen in the box provided. You should write one initial only for each answer. You will hear the piece twice.

[*pause*]

tone

Nonna: Hi, Ray.
Owen: Hallo Ray, something wrong?
Ray: Hi Nonna. Hell, this traffic. If they don't do something soon I'm going to find a job somewhere else!
Owen: Here, have a coffee.
Nonna: What is it today? The roundabout?
Ray: Thanks, Owen. Yeah, they've got to separate out the bikes on main roads. It's suicide in the rush hour. It wouldn't be difficult to make lanes at the side where cyclists'd be safe. On big roads, anyway.
Nonna: But there'd still be the juggernauts thundering alongside if they did that. Wouldn't it make more sense to have routes right away from the motor traffic?
Owen: Yes, but who's going to be prepared to cycle farther?
Nonna: Well, me, Owen, for one, if I felt safer.
Owen: But Nonna, you never go past the end of this road. It's energy you want, not safety. What people like you would really benefit from would be one of those schemes where you can park your bike or car on the outskirts and then get a cheap bus into the centre.
Nonna: Yeah, park and ride, aren't they usually called?
Owen: I think that's it, yeah.
Ray: I don't think people'd use it unless it was really cheap. Now if they were free …
Nonna: Oh, yeah, Ray very likely!
Ray: But if you didn't have to pay fares, everyone'd use the buses, then there'd be no congestion, bikes'd be safe …
Owen: Yes, but who'd pay for the buses?
Nonna: And who'd bother to bike if the bus was free?
Ray: People who needed to lose weight!
Nonna: Watch it, you!
Owen: But seriously, it would help if bus fares weren't so high. It would encourage more people to use them, don't you think?
Ray: Well, anything would help. You mean special fares for pensioners and so on?
Owen: Well, I was thinking if government put some money up, like they do in some countries, so the fares could be kept low.
Ray: I can see this lot doing that.

Owen:	And another thing is we need a lot more car parks ...
Nonna:	But where can we put them? Half the centre's a conservation area, they can't knock it down for car parks.
Owen:	But there's no reason why they shouldn't go under the centre.
Ray:	Plenty of other places have underground car parks.
Nonna:	Ugh. No. They always seem very sinister to me. And they'd cost a fortune to build.
Ray:	Well, if it costs a lot to park, people wouldn't bring cars into the centre, so that'd help too. I think that's a good idea. If you can afford a car you can afford to ...
Owen:	Don't be daft, Ray. Just because you haven't got one yourself. But I agree they would be costly to construct.
Nonna:	Well, I think it'd save a lot of hassle if they just kept vehicles out of the centre all together.
Ray:	Lovely, yeah, just turn the whole place into a great mall.
Owen:	Well, at least people'd still be able to shop there. It'll die if they don't do something soon.
Ray:	So what? We could leave it to the banks and the tourists. If the suburban railway was modernised, and subsidised ...
Nonna:	Yes.
Ray:	... and extended so it covered all the city, we could all get about easily ...
Nonna:	You're talking nonsense ...
Owen:	But where would you find space for new lines Ray?
Ray:	Where roads are now.
Nonna:	Ray, do be practical.
Ray:	Why not?
Owen:	Unless they put them underneath ... after all, you don't have to be a capital to have an underground ...
Nonna:	But, Owen, the cost would be horrendous!
Ray:	Yeah, of course.
Nonna:	Oh, come on, Ray!
Owen:	You're hopeless. Look, let's go down and get a take-away ...
Ray:	All right. But I'm right, you'll see, it'll take a while ...

[*pause*]

tone

Now you will hear the piece again. [The recording is repeated.]

[*pause*]

That is the end of Section C.

[*pause*]

Now look at Section D for the fourth and last part of the test. You will hear extracts of five different people talking. They are all talking about something to do with health. Look at Task One. Letters A–H list various different people. As you listen, put them in order by completing the boxes numbered 27–31 with the appropriate letter. Now look at Task Two. Letters A–H list the purposes of the people speaking in the extracts. As you listen, put them in order by completing the boxes numbered 32–36 with the appropriate letter. You will hear the series twice.

[*pause*]

tone

Student: Look, I'm really very sorry, but, well, I've got this awful headache, and my
             throat feels all kind of well, tender, when I swallow, I just can't think straight.
             So anyway I'm afraid the point is, well I haven't been able to do my
             assignment yet. I'm terribly sorry.

Surgeon: Now what we want to do, given that you're still bothered with this
             abdominal discomfort, and we haven't found anything in our tests which
             accounts for it satisfactorily, what we'd like to do, is, just make a small
             incision which would enable us to have a quick look round. It'd only take a
             few minutes, but I think it'd save you worrying. Don't you think that might
             be a good idea?

Parent: I'm sorry to bother you again, the thing is, you know you said I should call if
             her temperature rose, and it has and she seems to be breathing very fast.
             She had some of that medicine about an hour ago. Do you think I should
             give her some more, or had you better see her? I don't want to give you an
             unnecessary journey, but, well, she's so little, I don't like to take her out in
             this weather, not with such a high temperature.

Employer: I'm so very sorry to hear about your daughter. It must be very distressing
             for you. Now what I want you to understand is that when you need time to
             take her to the clinic for treatment or whatever, you are to take it. OK? I'm
             going to have a word with your line manager, so she can arrange cover. You
             don't need to ask permission every time. OK? We all feel for you about this,
             and we want to help however we can.

Dentist: Well, now I'm afraid it's a bit of a hassle, but I think the best thing for you to
             do, rather than have me writing letters and so on, which will only slow
             things up, is for you to contact the hospital yourself. Explain the problem
             with your jaw, tell them I've seen it and confirmed that it's not the teeth,
             they're all in reasonable condition, and see what they say. Then if they
             aren't helpful you can refer them to me and I'll see what I can do.

[*pause*]

tone

Now you will hear the piece again. [The recording is repeated.]

[*pause*]

*That is the end of Section D. There will now be a ten-minute pause for you to transfer
your answers to the separate answer sheet. Be sure to follow the numbering of all the
questions. The question papers and answer sheets will then be collected by your
supervisor.*

[*pause*]

That is the end of the test.

Practice Test 3

PAPER 1 READING (1 hour 15 minutes)

First text: 1 A 2 J 3 C 4 F 5 I 6 E 7 D 8 F 9 B
10 G 11 C 12 I 13 D 14 H

Teachers and students may be interested to know the books referred to in this text.

A: *Upland Britain* by Margaret Atherden (pub. Manchester University Press)
B: *Silent Spring* by Rachel Carson (pub. Houghton Mifflin 1962, Penguin 1991)
C: *Walks to Yorkshire Waterfalls* by Mary Welsh (pub. Cicerone Press)
D: *Cousteau's Great White Shark* by Jean-Michel Cousteau and Mose Richards (pub. Abrams)
E: *The Dammed* by Fred Pearce (pub. Jonathan Cape)
F: *Gaia: A new look at life on Earth* by James Lovelock (pub. Oxford University Press 1979)
G: *Whale Nation* by Heathcote Williams (pub. Random House UK)
H: *Standing on Earth* by Wendell Berry (pub. Golgonooza Press 1991)
I: *The Diversity of Life* by Edward O Wilson (pub. Allen Lane, The Penguin Press)
J: *The Amateur Naturalist* by Gerald and Lee Durrell (pub. Dorling Kindersley)

Second text: 15 B 16 B 17 A 18 A 19 B

Third text: 20 C 21 F 22 D 23 G 24 E 25 A

Fourth text: 26 B 27 C 28 D 29 F 30 H (all interchangeable)
31 B 32 C 33 F (all interchangeable)

PAPER 2 WRITING

See Study Notes p. 5 for general advice and Practice Test 1 Key p. 111 for sample plans and answers.

PAPER 3 ENGLISH IN USE (1 hour 30 minutes)

Section A

Question 1 [One mark for each correct answer]

1 D 2 B 3 A 4 A 5 D 6 B 7 A 8 C 9 D 10 C
11 A 12 D 13 B 14 C 15 D

Question 2 [One mark for each correct answer]

16 With 17 most 18 own 19 which 20 an 21 with 22 ever
23 for 24 who 25 of 26 Whether 27 out
28 is 29 may/could 30 by

Section B

Question 3 [One mark for each correct answer]

31 ✓ 32 rubbish. The 33 ✓ 34 clever,' said 35 it's 36 ✓
37 we think we 38 ✓ 39 physics 40 technologies, suggest
41 orbiting 42 tortoises. Only 43 may be

Question 4 [One mark for each correct answer]

44 be in 45 received/was given 46 longer 47 not renew/pay
48 continued 49 demand payment 50 ignored
51 a discount/reduction 52 legal 53 being treated 54 assurance

Section C

Question 5 [One mark for each correct answer]

55 A 56 K 57 B 58 J 59 C 60 D 61 G 62 F 63 E

Question 6 [These are specimen answers – up to two marks for each sentence]

81 It is the responsibility of your sponsors to organise and pay for travel to London.
82 Delegates will stay at the Atlantic Hotel, which is five minutes from Lancaster Gate underground station.
83 The cost of travel on the underground is refundable, but taxi fares are not.
84 Please check into the hotel between seven and nine p.m., identifying yourself as a language conference delegate in order to collect your meal vouchers.
85 The main conference centre is Merton Hall, which is situated on the corner of Merton Place.
86 If you are not familiar with London, please ask for directions from the hotel porter.
87 You should arrive at the Hall by 8.30 to allow time for administrative procedures, as the first session will start promptly at 9 a.m.

PAPER 4 LISTENING (45 minutes)

Section A [One mark for each correct answer]

1 passage 2 shoulder 3 word processor(s) 4 meeting room/area
5 photocopier 6 ceiling 7 wall/rack 8 external wall

Section B [One mark for each correct answer]

9 yes 10 no 11 yes 12 no 13 no 14 yes 15 yes 16 yes
17 no

Section C [One mark for each correct answer]

18 fury/outrage(d)/angry/furious 19 fair/just
20 optimism/see best in everything 21 bravery/courage/willing to take risks
22 let down/disappointed 23 guilty 24 cross/irritated
25 hurt/annoyed/resentful 26 his first wife's mother / his mother-in-law

Section D [One mark for each correct answer]

27 B   28 F   29 A   30 H   31 C   32 A   33 F   34 C   35 H
36 B

Transcript

This is the Certificate in Advanced English, Listening Test. Practice Test number 3. There are four sections to the test, A, B, C and D. You will hear Section B once only. All the other parts of the test will be heard twice. During the test, there will be a pause before each part to allow you to look through the questions, and other pauses to let you think about your answers. At the end of every pause you will hear this sound.

tone

You should write your answers on the question paper. You will have ten minutes at the end to transfer your answers to the separate answer sheet. The tape will now be stopped. You must ask any questions now, as you will not be allowed to speak during the test.

[*pause*]

Section A. Jim has called his business partner, Ed, to tell him about some ideas for altering their office. For questions 1–8, listen to what Jim says and complete Ed's notes. You will hear the recording twice.
[*pause*]

tone

Jim: Hi. Ed?
Ed: Jim. How're things?
Jim: I've been talking to that office design guy I told you about. He's made a lot of suggestions. I thought I'd relay them to you then you can make a few notes and mull them over, all right?
Ed: Sure.
Jim: Well, first of all, I think he's come up with a way to solve the space problem. He says, what we want to do, is knock down the inner wall of the passage, so we've got one big space. I said we'd thought of that but we didn't want clients bursting straight in on us, and he said, and I think this might work, that if the outer bit, like where they come in, if that was the meeting space, and the far end was our bit, so to speak, we could have a screen to keep us private. Sort of about shoulder height. Then we'd be able to pop our heads up and look, but our work space wouldn't be visible.
Ed: It might work.
Jim: Yeah. Yeah. Then he said if we had one big, like, work surface against the left wall, we could put the word processors on it as well as use it as ordinary desk space.
Ed: What about storage, though?
Jim: Well, we don't need the whole width of the room for the meeting area. We measured it, and he's right, we can easily fit a table and chairs in just over half. So we can have one whole wall in that part covered in deep cupboards.
Ed: Mm.
Jim: Yeah, and then there'll be a nice airy feeling where we work. And we can use the other wall, where the work surface isn't, for the telephone and stuff, and there'd be space for the photocopier along there too, which'd be really handy.
Ed: Won't it all be a bit dark and stuffy?

Jim: That's another thing we talked about. He said what we should do is rewire so we can have a light in the ceiling, and that could be centred over the table for meetings, right? But in the other half, like just above the, you know, work surface, we should have a rack of spotlights set in the wall so they shine on to it. And, and, to keep the place fresh we could have an extractor fan in the external wall. Well, don't you think he's got some good ideas? I told you he knew about these things.

Ed: Mm. Look, I've made some notes. I'll call you tomorrow when I've thought about them, OK?

Jim: OK, then. I'll wait till I hear, shall I?

[*pause*]

tone

Now you will hear the piece again. [The recording is repeated.]

[*pause*]

That is the end of Section A.

[*pause*]

Section B. You will hear a local radio announcement about travel conditions. For questions 9–17 look at the pictures and mark 'yes' the problems which are described. Mark the ones which are not described with 'no'. Listen very carefully as you will hear this piece only once.
[*pause*]

tone

Local radio announcer: ... and after the weather we have some information about travel conditions in the area today. Did you hear me say there wasn't much going on, earlier this morning? I take it all back. First of all, for those of you on foot, be prepared to go the long way round at the junction of Gale Street and the ringroad dual carriageway. Vandals have damaged the fencing of the elevated pedestrian walkway there and it has been declared unsafe, so you have to go right round the block at ground level and use the pedestrian crossing. Next, we have news that the airport is still having difficulties as a result of the torrential rain in the storm last week. Power has been restored by means of temporary cables, but pumping work is behind schedule so there is still an area of runway flooded. Services should be resumed tomorrow, but travellers should check by phone before leaving home. Another aftermath of the storm is that the bus stop in Bridge Street is still temporarily at the corner of John Street, as the fallen tree across the pavement has not yet been removed. New work is due to begin later today on the ring road approach to Park Street roundabout, and the road has already been closed. Diversion signs have been posted, but I should think you'd do well to avoid the park area entirely if you can, especially during this evening's rush hour. Lastly, if you're planning to use the car park at the corner of Station Road and Green Street – forget it. Apparently a lorry carrying scrap metal has shed its load right by the car park entrance and it's blocking it completely! What a mess! Well, after that, what we need is

some music, and I've got just the thing for all you travellers
with frayed nerves …

[*pause*]

That is the end of Section B.

[*pause*]

Section C. You will hear part of a radio programme in which James Clebourne, an award-winning photographer, talks to the presenter, Miranda Day, about his early life and the beginnings of his successful career. For questions 18–26, complete the information according to what James says. You will hear the piece twice.

[*pause*]

tone

MD: Hallo. This is Miranda Day, and with me on 'Talk Today' this time is James Clebourne. We've all enjoyed your photographs over the past twenty years or more, James. Did you come from an artistic family?

JC: Thank you, Miranda. Er, well, no I must say I didn't. Erm, I don't really remember my parents, who died in an air crash when I was three, but I think I can safely say that they weren't what is generally meant by 'artistic'.

MD: What sort of people were they?

JC: Well, as I said, I don't actually have any direct memories of them. Erm, they were well off. My father had what in those days was a very highly paid job, and my mother had money of her own. My infancy was charmed I think, er, you know, nanny and nurse maid and, er, the atmosphere of things being ordered for my benefit. It think it must have been that which caused the fury I felt at their deaths. Because I do recall that, although I don't remember them. I was just outraged. How could events have the temerity to turn on me and upset my world? That's how it was.

MD: And did the world change for you materially at that point?

JC: Yes, in fact it did. I had the silver spoon whipped smartly out of my mouth. Erm, my father's family wasn't rich, and his salary died with him. People didn't bother so much with life insurance in those days. Suddenly there was just my mother's pin money. I went to live with my father's brother and his wife. They were good people, schoolteachers, but quite different from my parents.

MD: In their attitudes as well as their style of life?

JC: Absolutely. They lacked the energy, the excitement of my parents and their friends. Rather puritanical, duty before pleasure, quite severe in their attitudes to human weaknesses. They made a good job of my upbringing though – erm, of course I suppose that's hardly for me to say, but you know what I mean – erm, I had to do as I was told. But they were scrupulously fair. One rarely had a sense of injustice about punishments for example.

MD: So do you think you inherited your personality from your parents, or can't you tell?

JC: Well, my father was always one to see the best side of everything, that's what everyone always told me who knew him. And that made him very positive in his work. I think I'm an optimist, that's one of the things that's helped me get on in my work. I guess we must have been quite alike in that.

MD: And your mother? Were your parents similar, do you know?

JC: Fairly, I should imagine. What I've always thought about her, is that she must've been quite brave, someone who would take risks. I suspect her family thought she took one when she married my father, and I guess I've taken a few over the years.

MD: In your career, you mean, for example?

JC: Yes. I don't say I'm a lot braver than plenty of other people. But one takes quite a bit of flak in a career like photography, especially if it's not the sort of thing one's family has gone in for.

MD: Did your family, your aunt and uncle, disapprove of your career choice?

JC: Erm, I suppose you could say that. I think my uncle, er, well, both of them, had hoped I would go to university and so on. But my uncle, he just sort of talked in a way, nothing direct, but he felt, er, obviously, I guess, a bit let down because, er, it wasn't what he'd hoped. Erm, but he didn't criticise me to my face.

MD: But your aunt?

JC: She said more. She minded that I hadn't taken their advice, and, er, made it abundantly clear in fact. And that lasted a long time.

MD: And you minded that?

JC: At first I did. I suffered terrible pangs of conscience that I had upset these people who'd been so good to me. Er, because they had, in their own way. As time went on and I began to make my mark in the field I'd chosen, I stopped feeling so guilty. Erm, I soon got back on terms with my uncle and just felt cross that they'd been holding something so unreasonable against me. It irritated me that they, at first, and latterly my aunt, should go on being so resentful after I'd been proved right. Erm, but that's a long way past, now, of course.

MD: You're still close?

JC: When I got married to my first wife, er, well that was a mistake, was one very good outcome in that I made a friend, my wife's mother, in fact, who is still a friend to me today. And before we got married, she took it into her head to sort out the bad feeling, er, said it would blight the marriage, etc. Erm, of course it was blighted anyway, we all found that out soon enough, but anyway, apart from her friendship, getting me and my aunt back so we trusted each other again, that was the best thing that happened around that marriage.

MD: And did it leave you scarred, the experience of a broken marriage, do you think, or ...

[*pause*]

tone

Now you will hear the piece again. [The recording is repeated.]

[*pause*]

That is the end of Section C.

[*pause*]

Now look at Section D for the fourth and last part of the test. You will hear extracts of five different people talking about a near disaster at an airport. A plane which was approaching the area had to make an emergency landing in poor weather conditions. The people are describing how the event affected them. Look at Task One. Letters A–H list various different people. As you listen, put them in order by completing the boxes numbered 27–31 with the appropriate letter. Now look at Task Two. Letters A–H list the main ideas expressed by the speakers. As you listen, put them in order by completing the boxes numbered 32–36 with the appropriate letter. You will hear the series twice.

[*pause*]

tone

Passenger: It was incredible, everything happened so fast, one minute we were in the air, the next we'd landed. To be honest I thought they'd just forgotten to do some of the routine things. None of us had any idea we'd been in danger till we were out on the ground. The crew were wonderful, they all knew just what to do, they kept calm and just made it all seem like part of the normal routine.

Restaurant manager: Well, what can we do? I can't have half a dozen extra waiters standing around every day on the off chance we'll have have a sudden rush, can I? These franchises are very tightly financed, we have to keep our costs right down or we can't operate. People complain enough already at the prices we have to charge, and if that means queues when there's been some sort of hold-up, there's not much we can do about it. I mean, contingency plans would mean staff on standby and as I say, we're not making the sort of profits that'd let us do that, are we now?

Pilot: Erm, I found, er, we had this problem, er, with one of the engines, so er, I contacted flight control again a bit sharpish, and er, they set it up, so I could go into the standard routine for such a situation, and erm, down we came. All very smooth luckily.

Customs officer: It was just chaos in here. They'd had so many flights on hold we just had this great stream coming through. We'd been standing around for hours, and half the shift had gone home, so there was no way we could do the usual number of searches. God only knows what they got through. It must have been a dream come true for the smugglers.

Steward: You know you go through it all so many times in your training, when you get to the real thing, it takes a while to cotton on that this is for real and there's actual danger and by then you're so busy it's just get through the work, get the passengers ready for emergency landing, make sure they're not panicking, keep looking calm, and before you know it, you're on the tarmac with shaking legs and you think, Wow! that would have been frightening if I'd had a chance to think about it.

[*pause*]

tone

Now you will hear the piece again. [The recording is repeated.]

[*pause*]

That is the end of Section D. There will now be a ten-minute pause for you to transfer your answers to the separate answer sheet. Be sure to follow the numbering of all the questions. The question papers and answer sheets will then be collected by your supervisor.

[*pause*]

That is the end of the test.

Practice Test 4

PAPER 1 READING (1 hour 15 minutes)

First text: 1 A   2 C   3 H   (1, 2 and 3 interchangeable)
4 F   5 G   (4 and 5 interchangeable)
6 B   7 C   8 E   (6, 7 and 8 interchangeable)
9 B   10 A   11 C   12 E   13 D
Second text: 14 C   15 A   16 D   17 B   18 C   19 A
Third text: 20 E   21 F   22 A   23 C   24 D
Fourth text: 25 E   26 A   27 D   28 B   29 F   30 B
31 C   32 D   33 F   (31, 32 and 33 interchangeable)
34 E   35 A   36 B   37 D   (35, 36 and 37
interchangeable)

PAPER 2 WRITING

See Study Notes p. 5 for general advice and Practice Test 1 Key p. 111 for
sample plans and answers.

PAPER 3 ENGLISH IN USE (1 hour 30 minutes)

Section A

Question 1 [One mark for each correct answer]

1 B   2 C   3 D   4 A   5 B   6 A   7 C   8 D   9 B   10 C
11 A   12 D   13 A   14 C   15 B

Question 2 [One mark for each correct answer]

16 even/still/much/far   17 to   18 you   19 up   20 whether/if   21 with
22 or   23 same   24 not   25 Some
26 while/but/whereas   27 worth   28 what   29 without   30 which

Section B

Question 3 [One mark for each correct answer]

31 his   32 √   33 so   34 if   35 feel   36 for   37 this
38 which   39 √   40 something   41 The   42 such

Question 4 [One mark for each correct answer]

43 overtime   44 good idea   45 didn't want   46 round/near
47 amount of / bit of   48 coming up   49 even though   50 against
51 no chance / no hope   52 a circle   53 got off   54 even though   55 piece
56 apart from / except for

Section C

Question 5   [One mark for each correct answer]

57 C   58 B   59 D   60 J   61 G   62 H   63 F

Question 6   [These are specimen answers – up to two marks for each sentence]

81   There is evidence that the pottery industry existed in the 14th century.
82   In the 17th century most of the pottery produced was for local use.
83   With the new fashion of tea-drinking came an increased demand for articles such as tea cups.
84   The 18th century saw the development of more refined pottery by Staffordshire potters such as Wedgwood and Spode.
85   Their designs showed the influence of recent excavations in Italy and imports from China.
86   At the same time, canals offered improved communications and Staffordshire pottery was exported.
87   Nowadays, Staffordshire pottery is still popular and commands high prices at auctions of antiques.

PAPER 4 LISTENING   (45 minutes)

Section A   [One mark for each correct answer]

1 North(ern)(of)   2 taking (it) apart/to pieces/bits
3 (working) petrol engine   4 steam   5 garden shed   6 kitchen (sink)
7 test engines/cars   8 engine   9 frozen lake   10 91.37

Section B   [One mark for each correct answer]

11 interpreter   12 Engineering   13 hotel   14 Communications
15 ceramics/pottery   16 Electronics   17 Friendship Store

Section C   [One mark for each correct answer]

18 B   19 D   20 D   21 A   22 B

Section D   [One mark for each correct answer]

23 A   24 B   25 F   26 D   27 E   28 H   29 F   30 E   31 A
32 B

Transcript

This is the Certificate in Advanced English, Listening Test. Practice Test number 4. There are four sections to the test, A, B, C and D. You will hear Section B once only. All the other parts of the test will be heard twice. During the test, there will be a pause before each part to allow you to look through the questions, and other pauses to let you think about your answers. At the end of every pause you will hear this sound.

tone

You should write your answers on the question paper. You will have ten minutes at the end to transfer your answers to the separate answer sheet. The tape will now be stopped.

You must ask any questions now, as you will not be allowed to speak during the test.

[*pause*]

Section A. For questions 1–10 you will hear a student telling her class about Henry Ford, the inventor. As you listen, complete the information in the notes. You will hear the recording twice.

[*pause*]

tone

Student: As part of my project on the development of the er, internal combustion engine, erm, I've been finding out about Henry Ford, who bears much of the responsibility for the early years. Well, he was born in 1863, in the northern United States. He was obviously of a mechanical turn of mind, he enjoyed messing around with farm machinery, taking it to bits and seeing how it worked and so on, even when he was just a kid. Anyway, he grew up, got married when he was in his early twenties, and erm, then he saw a working petrol engine and this really set him off. Because up till then, really, horseless carriages, well, that's what they were known as, were generally powered by steam, or sometimes electricity. What Ford did, was to harness the petrol engine to power a vehicle. He got a job with the Edison Electrical Company and at nights he worked, I think he was pretty obsessed really, so he er, worked in his garden shed. And, er, by the end of 1883, he'd managed to get his first rudimentary engine to fire and run, with his wife dripping in the fuel and him pushing the starting wheel, while it stood propped in the kitchen sink. And after that, there was no stopping him. By 1896, he'd got something he could drive about, which he called the er, Quadricycle, because it was basically a four-wheel bicycle, if you see what I mean, with an engine. In 1898 he started racing cars, he was going on building new ones, trying to improve them and he got into the racing so he could use it to test out what they could do. Well because he couldn't really push them to, you know, the limits on ordinary roads. The first one ever held in Detroit, he won, but it was really dangerous. His average speed was, er, forty-four point eight miles per hour, and he was doing that sitting on a seat right on top of the engine, and with no brakes. I think he must've been a bit mad. Anyway he went on, and, er, in 1904 he got the world speed record, and er, he was driving between banks of snow on a frozen lake, er on a track made of ashes to stop skidding, except it didn't all the time, but anyway, he did ninety-one point three seven miles per hour. I think that was pretty incredible. Anyway, meanwhile, the motor business was beginning to get organised …

[*pause*]

tone

Now you will hear the piece again. [The recording is repeated.]

[*pause*]

That is the end of Section A.

[*pause*]

Section B. You will hear a man confirming details of a business trip to China for his boss. For questions 11–17, complete the schedule for the trip. Listen very carefully as you will hear this piece only once.

[*pause*]

tone

Man: Hi, Janie, have you got the details for Margaret's China trip yet? [*pause*] Great, I'll get them down then. Now, she's flying to Hong Kong, then transferring, I've got the flights in the agency memo. And she's being met at Shanghai by a Mr Liu, right? Do we know who he is? [*pause*] Oh the interpreter? Well, that should be OK, at least he'll be able to talk English. That makes things easier. And he'll take her to wherever it is she's staying? [*pause*] Great. The Peace Hotel, like opposite of war? Fine. That'll be in the evening. What happens Wednesday then? She's got to go to a meeting at the university, hasn't she? Do we know where? [*pause*] I mean the university's probably got a lot of different departments, hasn't it? [*pause*] Oh, Engineering? Right, and how will she find it? [*pause*] I mean, has she got to be able to direct a taxi driver? [*pause*] So the hotel will see he knows where to go? Oh, fine. And then there's this lunch with some Committee? Communications Committee? [*pause*] Yes, that's what I thought. And then this Mr Liu is taking her to a Museum. Any idea what she'll see? [*pause*] Oh yes, she's very keen on pottery and paintings and things. That's nice of them. I imagine Chinese ceramics will be right up her street. And she's free in the evening, I expect she'll be glad to relax. She's got a long day on Thursday at this industrial place. Do we have a name for it? [*pause*] Well, if we don't know the Chinese, we'll put Electronics [*pause*] oh, that's what it is? This'll be the main meeting then. Will Mr Liu take her there, do you think? [*pause*] Uhuh. Eight o'clock from her hotel. Fine. And then Friday she leaves. What time'll she have to leave the hotel? [*pause*] Uhuh. So she can nip out and do a bit of shopping at the Friendship Store as long as she's ready to go by eleven? [*pause*] Uhuh. I'll tell her the Friendship Store's just by the hotel. Great. I'm sure she'll be relieved to hear it's all so well-planned. [*pause*] Thanks. See you.

[*pause*]

That is the end of Section B.

[*pause*]

Section C. You will hear an excerpt from a radio programme, 'Business Matters', in which Shirley, a woman whose business partner disappeared with all their money, discusses her experiences. For questions 18–22 you must choose the best answer A, B, C or D. You will hear the piece twice.

[*pause*]

tone

Presenter: … and now on 'Business Matters' we come to this week's case study. And this week we talk to Shirley Kildare, who has been through one of those nightmare experiences that we all think could only happen to others. Isn't that right, Shirley?

Shirley: Absolutely. It'd been such fun setting things up, and everything had been going really well, I mean, we started making a profit almost immediately, supplying these handmade chocolates to hotels and delis and so on, you know. I was quite surprised, I thought it'd take years to get known and so on, but we just caught a fashion. Anyway, when Nick did a bunk …

Presenter: He just disappeared?

Shirley: Just like that. I was devastated. How could he do it, I thought, after all our hard work together? I mean, we'd both worked hard, that was why I felt he was such a traitor, he'd let himself down, and he'd let me down.

Presenter: In different ways.

Shirley: Oh yes. To himself I suppose it was, well, it was a moral betrayal, but me, well, it was theft of course, literally, apart from everything else.

Presenter: What did he take?

Shirley: Everything. Absolutely every penny we had in the business. The bank account was empty. So I went straight round to the lawyers, and said, 'What can I do to get it back?' I had no idea …

Presenter: Was there nothing to be done?

Shirley: Well, no. Apparently not. We looked at the bits of paper, contracts and things, the lawyer was as horrified as I was. I still can't really take it in. But there you are. There was something we hadn't foreseen when we'd set the business up.

Presenter: So what did you do?

Shirley: What could I do? I sent the girls home from the workshop. I used what savings I had to help one or two of them who were most hard hit. Closed it up. Tried to sell the lease on the premises. My husband was in the States on a long contract. He offered to come back, but what could he have done? I was pretty depressed actually. My daughter wanted me to go to the doctor about it. I got through it though. One has to, in the end. There's an old lady who lives just up the road, she's all on her own, and I used to go and talk to her, just to give her company, and then one day I realised it was actually almost like a sort of therapy for me. You know, she was someone to lean on, to pour it all out to. I've got used to the idea, it's a closed chapter. I'm lucky not to have lost anything more than money. And a bit of self-esteem, I suppose.

Presenter: What about your partner? Have you given up hope of catching up with him?

Shirley: To be honest, I'm not sure I want to. I'd like my money back of course, but to have to face him again …

Presenter: Is it not a police matter?

Shirley: Oh, they did make quite strenuous efforts. We know where he left the country from, and they discovered a lot about him that we hadn't known, a few pretty unsavoury haunts, places he'd lived, businesses he'd been involved in, dicey accommodation addresses, that sort of thing. Where he's got to now, I haven't the foggiest. He might be back here living up the road for all I know!

Presenter: So what's next? Have you started anything new?

Shirley: Well – I've had a lot of good advice, a bit late most of it. I don't think I'll take on another partner, unless it was my husband or something! Actually, I'm still feeling pretty shattered, it's like convalescing from an illness really. I don't think I'm ready to call a halt completely, though. I, erm, well, I could retrain, get myself some more skills. But most probably I'll try and find myself a niche in someone else's company. And that'll help me relax a bit!

Presenter: Well, good luck Shirley, whatever you do. And thank you for sharing your experiences with us. Now let's turn to Bill Walters, our legal expert, and see what he has to say about ways of avoiding the problems that Shirley's encountered.

[*pause*]

tone

Now you will hear the piece again. [The recording is repeated.]

[*pause*]

That is the end of Section C.

[*pause*]

Now look at Section D for the fourth and last part of the test. You will hear extracts of five different people talking. They are all talking about some means of transport. Look at Task One. Pictures A–H show various different forms of transport. As you listen, put them in order by completing the boxes numbered 23–27 with the appropriate letter. Now look at Task Two. Letters A–H list the different feelings described by the people speaking in the extracts. As you listen, put them in order by completing the boxes numbered 28–32 with the appropriate letter. You will hear the series twice.

[*pause*]

tone

Elderly man:	It was like travelling with a maniac. He'd never used manual gears before, and he thought the speedometer showed kilometres, so we were going at these breakneck speeds. I was beside myself with terror. I almost wished a police car would appear! I've never been so grateful to get to the end of a journey.
Young woman:	How they're allowed to get away with it beats me. I mean, they charge enough. It's always too late or too early, the drivers don't know the routes. And you see in the paper all these profits they make, but they can't afford to get a new design that makes it easier to get on and off. I think it's disgusting. You can tell the bosses don't go to work on them – they'd never put up with it like we have to.
Child:	It was amazing. We started at this place, Angleside, which had everything just like it really was, with the porters and ticket men in old-fashioned uniforms, and there was a buffet with tea and cakes, no burger bars or anything. And they had funny little cardboard sort of tickets. And the engine was beautiful, and it all smelt really old-fashioned. And then we had this compartment all to ourselves, with luggage racks made of sort of netting. It was like something on telly. And when we went through the tunnel, they blew the whistle, and all this sooty stuff came in the windows.
Man:	I was doing fine till I discovered I'd left my wallet at the guesthouse. Well, there was nothing for it but to pedal all the way back. And nearly all uphill. I guess my legs were prepared for fifteen kilometres or so, but the trouble was we were more than halfway before I realised so it was more like twenty-five in the end. I was so shattered I could hardly totter through the door when we finally got home.
Woman:	It's just like part of a different world. Well, I guess that's what it is, isn't it? You just lay back and feel the breeze on your face. And you hear the birds, and the hooves on the track, and the rattle of the harness just every so often, as the driver flicks the reins. You wouldn't want to do it in bad weather, but it's the most peaceful thing going when it's fine.

[*pause*]

tone

Now you will hear the piece again. [The recording is repeated.]

[*pause*]

That is the end of Section D. There will now be a ten-minute pause for you to transfer your answers to the separate answer sheet. Be sure to follow the numbering of all the questions. The question papers and answer sheets will then be collected by your supervisor.

[*pause*]

That is the end of the test.

Part 4   The Speaking Test

STUDY NOTES

What happens in the Speaking Test?

The Speaking Test lasts for about fifteen minutes. You will take it with another candidate. When you go into the room, you will see two examiners. One of them will invite you to sit down and will make the introductions. The other examiner will not take part in the conversation except perhaps towards the end. To begin with, you will be asked one or two questions about yourself and your fellow candidate. If you know each other, you may be asked to tell the examiners about each other. If you don't know each other, you'll be invited to have a short conversation, finding out a bit about each other.

After about three minutes, the examiner will give you the first task. One of you will do most of the talking while the other listens. Then the examiner will give you both some different material and the other candidate has to talk while you listen. You each talk for about one minute.

The next part of the test involves both of you working together, discussing some pictures or information (there's very little to read) and trying to agree about them. It doesn't matter if you don't agree. The examiner will listen to what you say to each other for a few minutes and will then ask you a few questions to broaden the discussion. The other examiner may also join in at this point. At the end the examiners will tell you that the test is over and thank you. Then you can thank them and leave.

You'll find the atmosphere is quite relaxed and friendly. The examiners are there to help you to do your best. From their point of view, it's much pleasanter to give good marks than bad ones, so they will do all they can to encourage you. Remember to smile and greet them politely. During the test, say as much as you can and give opinions as well as facts. It's good to ask your partner's opinion too, at appropriate moments, because marks are given for turn-taking. But be careful, because you can lose marks if you try to dominate the conversation.

There are four phases in the test.

Phase A (about three minutes)

Introductions and general social conversation: The examiners will introduce themselves to you and then ask you to talk about yourselves, your work or studies, your plans for the future, your country or region etc. If you know your partner, you may be asked to talk about his or her background or interests. If you don't know your partner, you'll be asked to find out by asking questions, such as: Where are you from? Do you have a job or are you a student? Do you have any hobbies? etc. Try to avoid giving one word answers, but let a natural conversation develop, with each person both asking questions and giving information.

Phase B (about four minutes)

This phase is divided into two parts. In each part, one candidate is given something to talk about, while the other candidate listens, and, if necessary, asks a question or makes a comment at the end. You are expected to talk for about one minute each. You will probably have to describe a picture or group of pictures, while your partner compares what you are describing to the picture(s) he or she is looking at. There will be some differences which your partner may notice. For example, look at page C1 of the Colour Section. The examiner will ask one candidate to describe one of the pictures of ponds. The other candidate looks at page C2 and tries to decide which picture is being described.

If you're not sure exactly what you have to do, ask the examiner for clarification. For example you can say: *Please could you explain what we have to do again?* or: *I'm sorry, I don't quite understand what you want us to do.*

You won't lose marks by doing this. It's important to remember that there are no right or wrong answers during these discussions. The examiners are interested in your English, *not* your opinions! So don't worry about giving the 'right' answers, just make sure you speak as correctly, fluently and naturally as possible.

Phase C (about four minutes)

In this phase you will be asked to have a discussion with your partner. The examiner will give you something to look at together (for example, page C3, picture 1Q) and will ask you to discuss a subject connected with it. In the case of this example you are asked to discuss which foods are important in a balanced diet, and which are not. And remember – ask the examiner if you are not clear about what you have to do.

Phase D (about four minutes)

In this phase the examiner will probably ask you about your conclusions (if any) in Phase C, and then ask you questions to broaden your discussion. For example, after the discussion above, the examiner might ask about your own eating habits, or whether you think people worry too much about what they eat etc. Sometimes both examiners join in this part of the discussion.

At the end the examiners will thank you and tell you that the Speaking test is finished. The examiners are not allowed to give you any information about how well you've done, so don't ask!

THE TASKS

The best way to practise is with a friend. Try to avoid studying the Colour Section pictures too closely before you use them for practice. There are four sets of materials. For each practice session, you will need to go through the four phases described above. We have suggested some questions for each Phase A, but of course you can vary these to suit your circumstances.

Practice 1

Phase A

Ask each other questions about the area where you live, e.g.:
- What sort of area do you live in?
- Have you lived there all your life?
- What's good about living there?
- Are there any problems (e.g. transport, leisure amenities, shopping, employment opportunities)?

Try to chat naturally about these things for about two or three minutes.

Phase B

Part 1

Find pages C1 and C2 in the Colour Section. Look at one page each. Try to avoid looking at each other's pages. The person who has page C1 chooses one of the pictures and describes it for about one minute. The other person tries to guess which picture it is. At the end of the minute, the second person can ask questions if necessary. Then look at each other's pages and see whether you guessed right. It won't matter if you guess wrong – it's the speaker who's being examined, not the listener.

Part 2

Now change roles, so that the person who spoke in Part 1 becomes the listener, and the listener does the speaking. Look at pages C3 and C4. The person whose turn it is to speak should describe picture 1N while the listener looks at picture 1P and tries to find two things which are the same in both pictures and two things which are different. The listener can take notes if it helps. After about a minute, the listener tells the speaker what he or she thinks is the same or different. Then you can compare the pictures.

Phase C

Now look at picture 1Q on page 3C together. Talk together about the different foods you can see. Discuss which of these foods are important elements of a balanced diet and which are the least important. Discuss why. Say which of them you eat yourselves. Are there other essential foods missing from the picture? It doesn't matter whether you agree or disagree, provided you have a good discussion for about three or four minutes.

Phase D

At this point the examiner would join your discussion, if this was a real test. The examiner might ask you questions such as:
- Why is it important to think carefully about eating a balanced diet?
- Do you sometimes eat things which aren't good for you? Why?
- Do you think there are fashions in food?
- How do you think eating habits will change in the future?

Practise giving answers to these and any other questions you and your friend can come up with.

Practice 2

Phase A

Ask each other questions about studying English, e.g.:
- Where do you study?
- What sort of activities do you find most helpful?
- Do you have any particular reason for studying English?
- *(If you are in England)* How do you find living here helps your studies?

Try to chat naturally about these things for about two or three minutes.

Phase B

Part 1

Find pages C4 and C6 in the Colour Section. Look at one page each. Try to avoid looking at each other's pages. The person who has page C4 describes picture 2A for about one minute while the other person looks at picture 2B and tries to find three things which are different. At the end of the minute, the listener can ask questions if necessary. Then look at each other's pages and see whether you got it right. It won't matter if you get it wrong – it's the speaker who's being examined, not the listener.

Part 2

Now change roles, so that the person who spoke in Part 1 becomes the listener, and the listener does the speaking. Look at pages C5 and C7. The person whose turn it is to speak should describe picture 2C while the listener looks at picture 2D and marks the positions of the furniture on the office plan. After about a minute, the listener shows the speaker what he or she has marked and you can compare the picture and the plan. Remember, it doesn't have to be all perfect!

Phase C

Now look at picture 2E on page C7 together. Talk together about the gadgets shown. Discuss what they're used for and who might use them. How practical are they? Discuss whether you'd buy any of them for yourselves or as presents. It doesn't matter whether you agree or disagree, provided you have a good discussion for about three or four minutes.

Phase D

At this point the examiner would join your discussion, if this was a real test. The examiner might ask you questions such as:
- Are these gadgets things that people really need?
- Do people buy a lot of things they don't need? Why? Can you give examples?
- Do you think buying things we don't need is merely silly or is it harmful?
- What do you feel about the wasting of natural resources?

Practise giving answers to these and any other questions you and your friend can come up with.

Practice 3

Phase A

Ask each other questions about your aims and ambitions, e.g.:
- What are your plans for the future (your career, further studies etc.)?
- Have you always wanted to do this?
- What would you do if this was impossible?

Try to chat naturally about these things for about two or three minutes.

Phase B

Part 1

Find pages C5 and C8 in the Colour Section. Look at one page each. Try to avoid looking at each other's pages. The person who has page C5 describes picture 3A for about one minute while the other person looks at picture 3B and tries to find three things which are different. At the end of the minute, the listener can ask questions if necessary. Then look at each other's pages and see whether you got it right. It won't matter if you get it wrong – it's the speaker who's being examined, not the listener.

Part 2

Now change roles, so that the person who spoke in Part 1 becomes the listener, and the listener does the speaking. Look at pages C9 and C10. Pictures 3C and 3D both show a number of yoga positions. The person whose turn it is to speak should describe the five pictures in 3C while the listener looks at 3D where there are six pictures. The listener must try to spot which picture the speaker does *not* describe. The listener can take notes if it helps. After about a minute, the listener tells the speaker which one he or she thinks is the extra picture. Then you can compare the pictures.

Phase C

Now look at picture 3E on page C11 together. Imagine that you have been asked to choose one of these holidays to award as the prize for a competition for young writers. You must discuss which holiday would attract the most people to enter the competition. Explain to each other the reasons for your opinions. It doesn't matter whether you agree or disagree, provided you have a good discussion for about three or four minutes.

Phase D

At this point the examiner would join your discussion, if this was a real test. The examiner might ask you questions such as:
• Which holiday did you choose? Why?
• Would you enter such a competition?
• What sort of people would you expect to be travelling with if you went on one of these holidays?
• What effect do you think tourism might have on these places?

Practise giving answers to these and any other questions you and your friend can come up with.

Practice 4

Phase A

Ask each other questions about your country, e.g.:

(If you are in England):
• What are the main differences you notice between this country and your country?
(If your partner comes from another country):
• What can you tell me about your country?
• What are the main differences between our countries, do you think?
(If you are both in your home country):
• What foreign country would you particularly like to visit? Why?
• What do you like and dislike about living here?

Try to chat naturally about these things for about two or three minutes.

Phase B

Part 1

Find pages C6 and C12 in the Colour Section. Look at one page each. Try to avoid looking at each other's pages. The person who has page C6 describes picture 4A for about one minute while the other person looks at picture 4B and tries to find three things which are different. At the end of the minute, the listener can ask questions if necessary. Then look at each other's pages and see whether you got it right. It won't matter if you get it wrong – it's the speaker who's being examined, not the listener.

Part 2

Now change roles, so that the person who spoke in Part 1 becomes the listener, and the listener does the speaking. Look at the pages C8 and C12. The person whose turn it is to speak should describe picture 4C while the listener looks at picture 4D and tries to decide how the two pictures are related. After about a minute, the listener tells the speaker how he or she thinks the pictures are related. Then you can compare the pictures.

Phase C

Now look at the headlines at the bottom of page C9 together. Imagine that these are headlines from newspapers ten years in the future. What might be the consequences if any of them were true? Discuss which one would be the most exciting news. It doesn't matter whether you agree or disagree, provided you have a good discussion for about three or four minutes.

Phase D

At this point the examiner would join your discussion, if this was a real test. The examiner might ask you questions such as:
- Which headline did you choose as the most exciting? Why?
- Do you think that solving one problem might lead to new ones?
- What do you think is the most serious problem facing people in your part of the world?
- Do you have any ideas about how it could be solved?

Practise giving answers to these and any other questions you and your friend can come up with.

Sample answer sheet for Paper 1

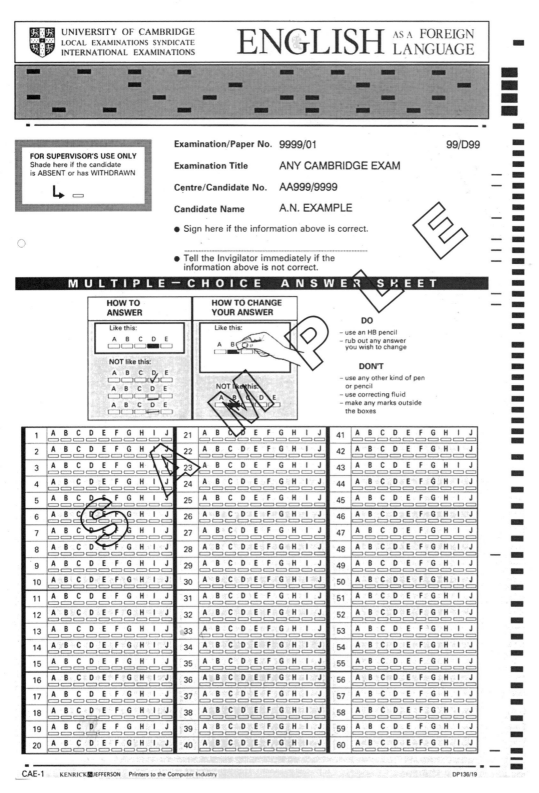

© UCLES/K&J

151

Sample answer sheet for Paper 3 (first sheet)

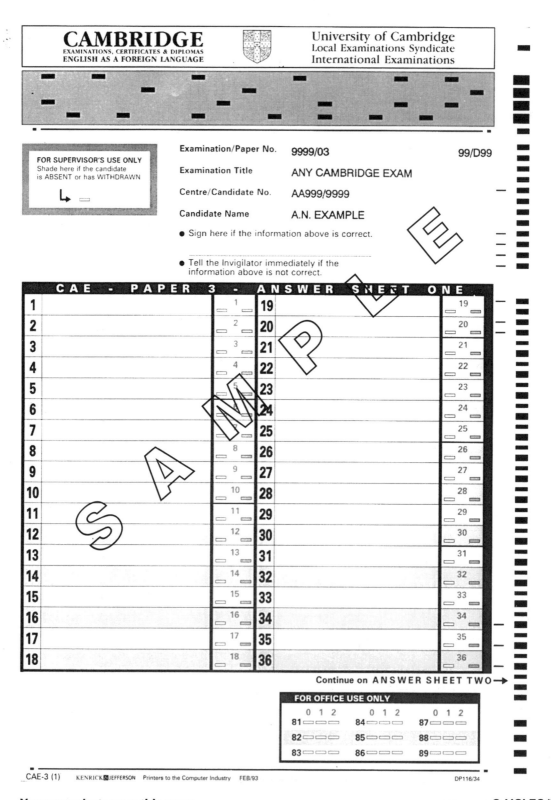

© UCLES/K&J

Sample answer sheet for Paper 3 (second sheet)

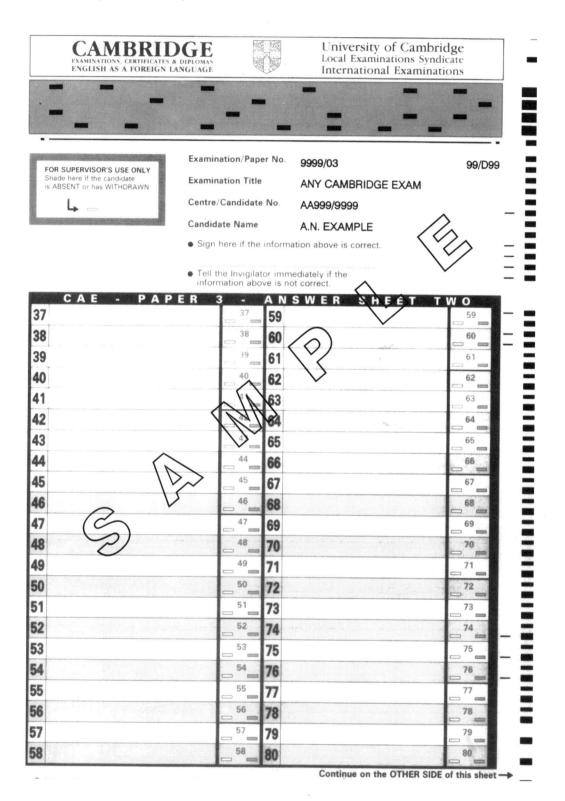

You may photocopy this page.

© UCLES/K&J

Sample answer sheet for Paper 3 (second sheet - reverse side)

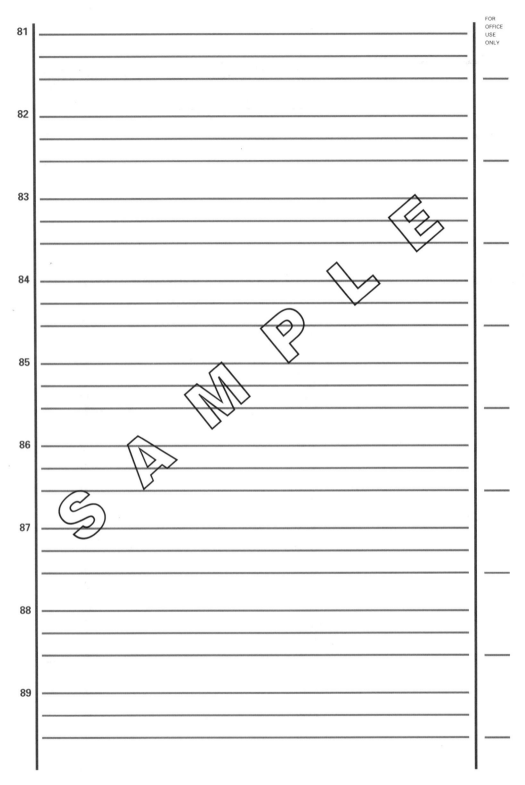

81

82

83

84

85

86

87

88

89

© UCLES/K&J

Sample answer sheet for Paper 4

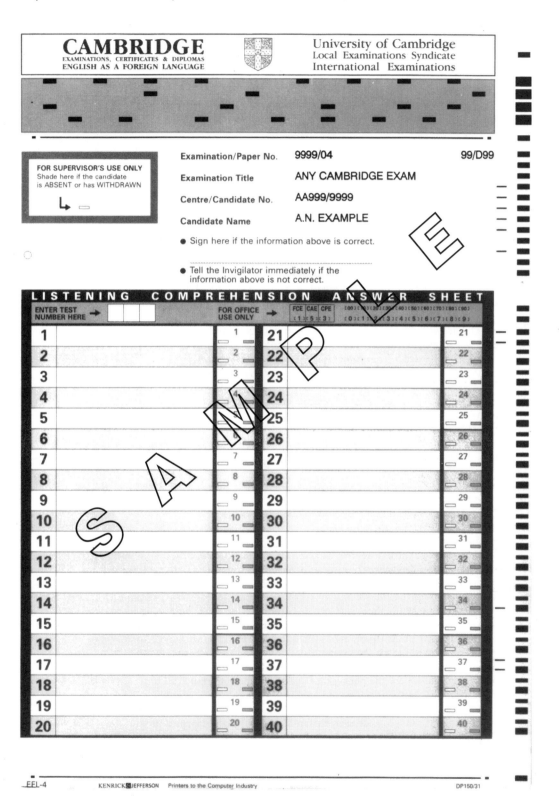

You may photocopy this page.

© UCLES/K&J

155

Acknowledgements

The sample answer sheets are reproduced by kind permission of the University of Cambridge Local Examinations Syndicate.

The author and publishers are grateful to the following individuals and institutions who have given permission to reproduce copyright material. It has not been possible to identify the sources of all the material used and in such cases the publishers would welcome information from copyright owners.

The Museum of Modern Art, New York for the extracts from the National Gallery of Art's *Winter 1991 Film Calendar* (p. 19); *The Independent* for extracts by the following journalists: Malcolm Smith (p. 21), Danny Danziger (p. 23), Sabine Durrant, Peter Gutteridge and Nick Caistor (p. 49), Robert Winder (p. 50), James Gleick (p. 67), Anne Daniel (p. 88); News team for the photograph (p. 89); Still Pictures for the photograph (p. 21); Raymond Blanc for the photograph (p. 23); The Kobal Collection for the photograph (p. 27); the following publishers for the use of jacket artwork: Harvill, an imprint of HarperCollins Publishers Limited for *The Year of The Death of Ricardo Reis* by José Saramago; Serpent's Tail for *Makbara* by Juan Goytisolo; Bildarchiv for *The Palace of Dreams* by Ismail Kadare (p. 50); Duncan Petersen Publishing Limited for the extract from *Charming Small Hotel Guides: Italy* (p. 25); A & C Black (Publishers) Limited for the extract from *Blue Guide to the Channel Islands* by Peter McGregor Eadie (p. 30); Random House for the extract from *The Vegetarian Epicure* by Anna Thomas (p. 32); Coronet, an imprint of Hodder & Stoughton Limited for the extract from *Supernature* by Lyall Watson (p. 33); Chatto & Windus for the extract from *Culture and Society 1780–1950* by Raymond Williams (p. 35); *Women and Home* for the extract (p. 42); Allsport for the photographs (pp. 42 and 70); © William Boyd for the extract published in the *Daily Telegraph* (September 1990) (p. 44); Harrington Kilbride for the extracts from *Healthcare* (pp. 46 and 100); Kelloggs for the illustration (p. 47); *The Literary Review* for the extract (p. 54); Macmillan Publishers Limited for the extract from *Through Britain on Country Roads* by Peter Brereton (p. 56); University Botanic Garden, Cambridge for the extract (p. 57); © Jeremy Ripkin for the extract from *Bovine Burden*, published in *Geographical Magazine* (July 1992) (p. 59); *BBC Wildlife Magazine* for the extracts (pp. 65, 66 and 72); Ian Whadcock for the illustration of 'The Monotony Tree' (p. 72); *Green Magazine* and *Country Living* for the extracts (pp. 65 and 66); Mark Allen Publishing Limited for the extract from *Splash* a supplement of *Outdoor Action* (p. 69); Usborne Publishing for the extract from *Understanding Modern Art* by Bohm-Duchen and Cook (p. 77); Transworld Publishers Limited and Writers House for the extract from *A Brief History of Time* by Stephen Hawking (p. 78); Penguin Publishers for the extract from *The English Novel* by Walter Allen (p. 81); *BBC Music Magazine* for the extract (p. 90); *The Independent on Sunday* for the extract by Sam Wauchope (p. 92); The National Magazine Company Limited for the extract from *Good Housekeeping* (March 1993) (p. 94); Cedar Halls Health Farm for the photograph (p. 96); W. Foulsham & Company Limited for the extract from *Adventure Weekend* by Alan Pearce (p. 101); Cassell plc for the extract from *Opera* by Carole Rosen (p. 102); Bloomsbury Publishing Limited for the extract from *The Language of Clothes* by Alison Lurie (1992) (p. 104); Jeremy Pembrey for the photograph (p. 144); The University of Cambridge Local Examinations Syndicate for OMR sheets (pp. 151–155).

In the colour section, pages C1–C12, photographs 1A–M are by Jeremy Harpur; photographs 1N, 1P, 1Q, 2A, 2B, 2C, 3A, and 3B are by Jeremy Pembrey; photographs 4A and 4B are by Rex Features Limited; photographs and text in 2E are from Innovations Mail Order and are reproduced by kind permission of NSP Catalogue Holdings plc; the plan in 2D is by Peter Ducker; photograph 4D is by Stephanie Colasanti; pictures in 3C and 3D and the headlines in 4E are by Abbas; holiday adverts in 3E are by Peter Ducker with additional artwork by Leslie Marshall and HardLines; photograph 4C is by Barbara Thomas.